the pursuit of
xceptional execution **Kevin Kelly**

DO! THE PURSUIT OF XCEPTIONAL EXECUTION

An Inspiring Irish Publications Book

The moral right of the writer has been asserted.

ISBN 978-0-9541868-9-0

Copyright 2013 by Kevin Kelly, Poilini, Furbo, Co. Galway, Ireland
www.kevinkellyunlimited.com

Copyright Information All rights reserved. No parts of this book may be reproduced or
transmitted in any form or by any means, electronic, mechanical, photographic or
phonographic process, nor may it be stored in a retrieval system, or otherwise be copied for
public or private use -- other than for "fair use" as brief quotations embodied in articles and
reviews -- without prior written permission of the copyright holder and publisher.

CONTENTS

ACKNOWLEDGEMENTS

Wow! This has been an amazing journey unlike any of my previous experiences at writing a book. I learned beyond all reasonable doubt the power of assembling a fantastic team who challenges you, provokes your boundaries, and ultimately raises your performance beyond anything you imagined. In completely random order, a heartfelt thanks to our book team.

Huge gratitude to the xceptional Tim Sanders and Net Minds team, a brilliant disruptive start-up transforming the world of publishing. Thank you for your friendship and sage guidance throughout this journey.

Project Manager Gary Percy risked all to challenge me every moment of this journey. Thank you for your incisive inquiries and superb organization.

My hugely talented collaborator, Developmental Editor Adam Wren. Thanks a million for setting the standards and raising the bar higher than I thought I could jump.

Designer Ute Christopher, thanks for superb creative contributions.

Consulting Editor Brian Solon, you transformed the book in epic proportions.

To my friend and proofer, Eileen Bennett, a sincere thanks for your work throughout the years.

The Xceptionalists who prove that the busiest and brightest people can be grounded as well. Thank you for the stimulating conversations we shared and I look forward to your new ventures.

And my inner circle:

My wife Deirdre for her faith and love.

Our son Conor, our little superstar, to whom this book is dedicated.

My parents Kevin and Mary who encouraged my evolution.

My friend Gary Loughlin, a brilliant videographer who continues to go beyond the call of duty.

All my family and friends throughout the world for your inspiration.

1
XCEPTIONAL EXECUTION OF AN ORDINARY IDEA

What if launching and leading an xceptional business was simpler than you've ever imagined? Not easier. Not less time consuming. Not less gut wrenching, but simpler. Guess what: It is. What if I told you many successful entrepreneurs didn't start with a compelling vision or indeed a workable business plan? Guess what: That's true too. What if it was possible to dominate a market without any previous background in it? Well? It is.

Xceptional execution is about taking a relatively simple idea from brainstorm to breakout hit. Groundbreaking research conducted by Columbia University's Amar Bhidé in 2000 titled *The Origin and Evolution of New Businesses* reinforced the term's significance, revealing that 88 percent of 'breakthrough companies' were the result of 'exceptional execution of an ordinary idea' according to their owners. Only 12 percent were the result of new inventions.

Amar told me that while some factors have changed since he first published his findings, for example, access to capital is more widespread through crowdfunding, along with a mainstream popularization of entrepreneurship and rise of a global start-up ecosystem, these developments haven't changed the fundamental principle of his work.

You don't have to be Bezos or Branson, Einstein or Jobs. Your product doesn't have to be a Bentley, Hublot or a Stradivarius. And your product or service doesn't have to be a Dropbox, a Flickr or a Hulu. You must simply find an ordinary idea and implement that idea with xceptional execution.

How do I know? In a few words – my lifelong bent towards doing and executing. Growing up in a small town on the west coast of Ireland, I began life in my family's business Kelly's Store selling gas and groceries at the age of six. Over the next dozen years I sold to every imaginable type of person on the planet. From a customer who wanted to share their life story with me, the listening six year old, to a customer who wanted speed and efficiency at all costs.

Following college, I worked for three years in marketing for manufacturing and construction companies, breaking each of their sales records before deciding to found my own firm, Advanced Marketing, in 1990. There I worked with SMEs who produced everything from ambulances to hand-carved wooden staircases and high-end wrought iron gates.

One of my overseas adventures brought me to Africa where I built schools, and trained teachers and students in the Mukuru slums of Nairobi. Following on from this, I became a consultant to multinational businesses and advisor to start-ups on growth strategies.

On my travels, I've had the fortune to meet some of the finest business minds on the planet: The Xceptionalists. Hailing from around the globe, they lead some of the world's most compelling brands and companies, from one to 3,000 employees and a range of revenues from $100k to $130million.

In this book, you can learn from the people who live and breathe the xceptional execution ethos. Talking with the Xceptionalists, I delve deep into their souls to highlight the entrepreneurial DNA and thinking underpinning their success.

The Xceptionalists lay to rest the myth that a visionary with a carefully prepared business plan will thrive or even survive in the real business world. They are entrepreneurs from Buenos Aires, Argentina to Bologna, Italy, from Des Moines, USA, to Galway, Ireland, who run app companies, consultancies, clinics and sprawling technology corporations. Authentic doers who tackle fear and think for success, offering practical tips and daily rituals to help you achieve the xceptional execution of your idea.

THE XCEPTIONALISTS

Asthma Care – Galway, Ireland

Ordinary idea: Nose Breathing

Xceptional execution: Using this basic skill to build profitable niches in snoring, high performance athletics, asthma and more.

Balsamiq – Bologna, Italy

Ordinary idea: Whiteboarding

Xceptional execution: In five years, from zero to 150,000 customers and $6 million in sales. Single founder, bootstrapped, distributed team.

Blo Blow Dry Bar – Vancouver, Canada

Ordinary idea: Hairdrying

Xceptional execution: Branding brilliance that has seen the franchise move from Canada to the US and now into the Far East.

Business Model You – Portland, USA

Ordinary idea: Career Coaching

Xceptional execution: From career planning to career modeling.

Dwolla – Des Moines, USA

Ordinary idea: Commerce

Xceptional execution: On target to change the way we process payments all over the globe. Has the potential to eliminate credit cards from our pocket.

Globant – Buenos Aires, Argentina

Ordinary idea: Software development

Xceptional execution: In 10 years the firm specialized in the creation of innovative software products, grew from four founders to 3,000 employees, receives 1,600 resumes a month and creates software for top tech companies like Google, Electronic Arts and LinkedIn.

Outfit7 – Limassol, Cyprus

Ordinary idea: Talking Tom Cat

Xceptional execution: Embracing the fun factor and getting into people's hearts with their characters, they've surpassed 1 billion downloads.

Unislim – Newry, Northern Ireland

Ordinary idea: Weight loss

Xceptional execution: Ireland's longest-running slimming club, outlasting all fad diets, gimmicks and the latest 'Miracle Cure' on the market with 300 weekly classes throughout the country.

WeDemand — Rio de Janeiro, Brazil

Ordinary idea: Concerts

Xceptional execution: Crowdsourcing and crowdfunding platform bringing over 65 international bands to Brazil, selling over 63,000 tickets and creating invaluable resources for promoters, bands and fans.

2
CONFESSIONS OF AN IDEA KILLER

Hi, my name is Kevin and I used to be an idea killer.

For almost a decade, my job was to detonate concepts for new small businesses before they reached the launch pad. Yes, to stop potentially great ideas before they got to market. Now, that wasn't the title on my business card, but if it were, it would've been accurate.

Officially, I was a Feasibility Consultant: Clients brought me ideas for new small and medium-sized ventures. My job, in turn, was to prepare a fancy, high-minded report analyzing whether the new business would fail or succeed.

For $10,000 a pop, I exhaustively analyzed dozens of business ideas over the years for recreational centers, boutique furniture businesses and plans for a shop purveying fine crystal. Some may have never made it. Some could have become global brands. The truth is, when I dashed these entrepreneurs' dreams, I didn't know any different.

I did know how to say 'no' though. Here's how I would kill your idea: You ask me to evaluate your new venture. We sit down at a nice coffee shop together here in Ireland, just steps from the Atlantic Ocean, and you pitch.

Maybe you pitch a game changing, industry busting and ruckus-causing whopper of a start-up. You tell me about your proposed revenue streams and about all the reasons why your start-up will succeed. It has a distinctive, creative culture, plan for employee engagement and is focused on the connection economy. Your new venture ticks off all the buzz boxes.

Then I go away and find enough reasons why this venture cannot possibly succeed. Not intentionally, of course, but unfortunately that was the normal outcome.

The list of why-you-shouldn't is endless. A product of that kind already existed. It existed longer than your concept, had more brand recognition and market share. It was difficult to see how you can compete and make this work. If it's a truly new product, then there's no market for it, and no market means no demand, and no demand means no sales, and no sales means no profits.

A few weeks later I share my insights. Sipping my latte, looking out over the peaceful sea through the window behind you with a sparkle in my eyes, I turn to you and render my verdict: "Your business will fail." To each of the game changing businesses introduced in this book I would have issued the same prognosis: failure.

To end my infamous idea killing session, I back up my argument with a 60-page report. Though I couch the outcome in jargon and niceties, the verdict is almost always the same. It – whatever the it is – can't be done. Can you imagine what I would have say to those that turned up with no industry knowledge? No compelling vision? No business plan? I would have, for example, told Ben Milne of Dwolla that his idea had no potential.

All Ben had was a burning desire to solve an existing problem. His company was paying too much in credit card fees. When Ben first shared his vision of changing the way people send and receive mobile payments with others, the question posed to him was, "Why?" Why the need for Dwolla, when the system is working just fine? Good question. His answer came in the form of a product that poses a $1 million-a-day challenge to companies such as Visa and MasterCard. Ben says, "Actually, Kevin, the current system is not working just fine."

The man who founded Dwolla and is changing the face of the financial world had no prior background in the industry before he began in 2009. Four years later, Forbes magazine listed Ben Milne from Dwolla as one of the 12 most disruptive names in business for his groundbreaking idea of helping customers process a transaction in a simpler way.

If four Argentinian business people had called me about wanting to make their country a technology hub during a financial crisis when the peso was devalued, I would have swiftly shown them the exit door. I didn't need to hear that they had no business plan, the country had no history in technology, and they had only $5,000 in capital. Those four entrepreneurs started Globant, now a global company with 3,000 employees and revenues of $129 million.

And what about the lady who admitted in her first class that she hadn't got a clue about how to lose weight? Would it have been worth the gas driving to see me? Agnes McCourt, now 72, created Unislim, Ireland's biggest slimming organization. It is now over forty years in existence and continues to grow and evolve.

These are not isolated stories. 40% of Inc. 500 founders that were interviewed in Amar Bhide's book had no past experience of working in the industry they went on to dominate. A survey of Inc. 500 entrepreneurs found 60% didn't create a business plan before launching their companies.

After years of naysaying, I've learned some very important lessons. The most important one is: It's not about the idea. It's not about the business plan or the compelling vision to kickstart the process. It's all a little less complicated than that. And it's not about an occasional success or failure either, it's about the entrepreneur behind those successes and failures.

It's about the xceptional execution of that ordinary idea.

XCEPTIONAL EXECUTION

The antidote for too much knowledge is execution. Why? Execution helps to work through fear and builds confidence. Knowledge will always give you enough reasons not to act. Execution is taking the next step in spite of that knowledge. Xceptional execution is taking that next step with your decisions underpinned by clarity and understanding.

What follows is advice on how to deal with people like me: (former) idea killers. It's about how to deal with the idea killer in your own head, the part of your brain where fear and knowledge keep you from executing the brilliant ideas your mind generates every day. And it's about developing entrepreneurs like you into the kind of people for whom the xceptional execution of their ordinary idea becomes part of their DNA.

My goal is to get you to execute one of your ideas in a truly exceptional way. You'll always have enough reasons not to act, not to DO! Not enough time, not enough money, not enough support from those you think you need support from, not enough will or skill. But what matters isn't what you lack. What matters isn't your idea. What matters is what you DO! What will you DO?

This is unquestionably the advice of an ordinary man, who others describe as nothing more than an authentic, passionate person with an insatiable appetite for learning. I'm no guru or thought leader, I'm a doer. After years of telling people like you the opposite, whatever you have in mind, it can be done.

Xceptional execution brings results. To launch and lead a breakthrough company you don't need to invent the next light bulb. You don't need $50,000 in the bank. You can start with what you have, exactly where you are.

3
THE FEAR FACTOR

AUSSIE RULES

The journey to Melbourne was unpleasant. Unshaven and dressed in shabby tracksuit bottoms, I wandered towards my appointed meeting spot on Chapel Street, a district known for its fine dining and shopping experience.

It was the morning after the night before, and empty wine bottles and other remnants of trash adorned the walkway. With each step, the brick in my stomach seemed to gain mass and weight. I did not want to go where I was headed, and once I arrived, I did not want to do what I was supposed to do.

Contrary to my usual headlong rush into new challenges, I stopped and rested for a few moments, sitting on a nearby stoop of a dilapidated building, trying to wrap my mind around the task ahead: Begging for the day's wedges.

It was the early 90's, and I was visiting Australia as part of my lifelong study on human behavior – specifically I was attempting to understand the source of personal energy.

I wanted to know the source of my passion, energy and enthusiasm. Was I wired differently? Financially I didn't need to beg, I was gratefully doing well. Emotionally and psychologically

21

however, I needed to overcome some fears.

After completing my rest on the stoop, I knew I couldn't procrastinate any more. To begin, I found a moderately trafficked spot. I thought, 'Perhaps I should attempt a practice run.'

I extended both my hands out, palms down. Even pretending to beg was terrifying. At that moment an elderly woman was walking my way. 'Easy, I can do this', I thought. 'Now all I have to do is...'

Yet I couldn't even look at her. Twisting my hands into the proper begging position felt impossible. Ten or fifteen minutes passed, but the squeamish feeling remained.

The challenge was too much for me, but why? After all, this was Melbourne, Australia, and I was Kevin Kelly from Ballintubber, Ireland – a sleepy village in the West of Ireland with two bars, a shop, a school, a post office and historic ruins. Ballintubber was a dot on the map, not a destination.

Nobody knew me here. This was the perfect begging environment for an Irish, habitually Armani-suited businessman. None of that seemed to matter because some mysterious power had gripped me: Fear! Just then, I noticed my buddy, Chris, in the distance.

"Well, you aren't going to make much money with your hands in that position," he said to me. "I can't do it," I moaned. 'Can't do' was, until this moment, a two-word phrase not present in my daily vocabulary.

"Yes, you can." Chris fired back. "Look, I've got two dollars already."

Although I was grateful for the encouragement, his words had the anything but the desired effect. His success as a beggar really sickened me. If he had failed as well, at least we could have moaned together.

As this silly scene played out, I butted up against one of the grand dilemmas of the human experience and encountered a choice: Expose myself to potential failure or maintain my self-image. Was the potential dent to my ego from failing – greater than the negative impact of begging?

"Get up and ask people!" Chris commanded. "What do you say to them?" I asked Chris, in hope of discovering some sort of secret verbal formula for performing the task with success. "Can you give me some money?" he replied.

Ugh, not what I was hoping for. Summoning my last reserves of courage, I stood up. Within seconds, I had walked right past three people. Words were not coming easily. Finally, having backed myself into a corner, I resigned myself to taking action. Without a second thought, I approached an elderly man.

"Can I have some money, please?" I enquired. "No," came his stern reply, and he had barely left the scene when I started to laugh. I laughed so much it hurt. It was a laughter mixed with delight and despair. Delight, because it felt like a huge boulder had been lifted off my shoulder. Despair, because some people just aren't nice, and begging certainly isn't good for your health. With renewed energy, I proceeded to ask four other people for donations but they all refused to give as much as a cent. So much for the Australian bond with the Irish.

When it was time to reconvene with my friends, I discovered that Zack, Diana and Chris – all fellow course participants – had all been given money. I had nothing to report. "How the bloody hell did you get so much?" I enquired.

Zack had got over six dollars from telling people the whole story of who he was, where he was from, and the theme of the exercise: 'The death of the ego'. Remembering the old saying that 'if you keep doing what you are doing, you'll keep getting what you've got', I decided to adopt Zack's strategy.

While my friends went off to give their money away, I kept on the scent of my first dime. I approached a group of young people and insisted on telling them the story, following up with the usual request for money. I was rewarded with another negative response.

Pride gone, I pleaded with them. "Fifty cents, twenty cents, ten cents, anything please," I said. Not a cent came. I began to realize for the first time in my life what it must feel like for those who are forced to beg in order to subsist. This experience was the catalyst for a major change in my attitude towards these courageous people. On my way back to the car, remembering I had brought some money with me for a cup of coffee, I took ten dollars out of my pocket and gave it to a beggar who was sitting nearby. I was forever changed.

On that warm, humid day in Melbourne I learned that our pride, our ego and our fear of failing often keep us from achieving greatness, keeping us stuck in jobs we don't like, working with people we can't stand, engaging in pursuits we're not wholeheartedly passionate about. They all prevent us from discovering happiness, leading lives full of meaning and offering our art to the world.

That day I faced my greatest fears – the fear of being humiliated and the fear of failing. This wasn't about the money. It was about me having the guts to beg and feel like a piece of shit in everyone's eyes. It was about getting over my ego in the knowing that I'm much more than this. It was about knowing that failure is okay as long as you learn and grow from it. That day I grew six feet.

BIGGEST LIE IN BUSINESS

Half of all new businesses fail after their first five years. The lie we propagate is that if you start a business, it has a coin toss chance of going belly up. Thousands of potential entrepreneurs strike out on their own, launch their idea, and fall on their ass. Chastened by their experience, they return to their former boss and old way of life, back to following the rules.

These failures are neither final nor fatal. Many of those

entrepreneurs, awakened to a kind of freedom they've never experienced before, learn from their failure and go on to launch a business that thrives. How do entrepreneurs survive their early failures? They don't view their failures as failures. They view these experiences as feedback, and a prelude to future success.

Ben Milne of Dwolla says, "You know I have had about fifty failures already today. The fact is I have failed in making adaptions to the product. In the past, I have failed at selecting business partners. I nearly went out of business three times in my career. When you are failing the key point is to just admit it. Remember you still have a shot after you fail. The longer you drag it out the less chance you have."

In business, failure isn't always a big problem according to Peldi from Balsamiq. "Mistakes don't really matter that much as long as you fix them straight away and put your hand up. There might be some tough love at the start but if you fix the problems you will be fine. It is very much the lean start-up way: throw it out there and listen. Don't be afraid of shipping something you aren't fully proud of yet. On three occasions over the last few years, we published a bad build. Immediately we apologized on our blog and worked to fix it. The ironic thing is it got picked up by some site that cited it as the 'Apology of the Week'."

Why fear feedback? Why stigmatize failure in the workplace when it's bringing you closer to achieving your organizational goals. If you want to find the next big success, feedback comes with the territory.

FEAR AS FUEL

How do you deal with fear? Many of the Xceptionalists appeared to have a common approach: Most honor it and see it as their teacher. Without it you could become complacent. After reflecting on the source of their fears, they take action. It might be to mitigate the risk or prepare even better but in all cases, decisive action is taken that moves them closer to their goal.

FACING YOUR FEARS

In the early 1970's, during the height of the political turmoil that rocked Northern Ireland, Agnes McCourt, owner of Unislim had to face her biggest fear. One Monday she received a call from a client wondering why they had cancelled their class. After being unsuccessful in their attempts to contact the class leader, Agnes and her husband decided to travel to the venue, a Unionist Hall in a local town.

That night, close to the venue, a man dressed in a balaclava with gun in hand approached the car asking about their travel plans. When he became aware of who they were, he pointed the gun at Agnes's husband, Brian, and suggested that they leave the area immediately. They were reminded of what had happened to the Miami Show Band, a popular cabaret band from Dublin who were killed by a paramilitary group from Northern Ireland years before in a nearby area.

Shaken and scared, they returned home via a different route. On arrival, Agnes rushed into the house, up the stairs and into the children's room, hugging each one of them as she thought about the fate that could've befallen her. Shortly after, every Unionist Hall Committee cancelled their Unislim classes. On another day, protesters in Portadown carried placards that advised the public not to support Dunnes Stores or Unislim. Why was this happening?

The Unionists believed them to be Irish Republican Army sympathizers. As they travelled through that dark valley, Agnes's husband wanted to cease all business links in Northern Ireland and relocate to Southern Ireland.

Agnes agreed to the house move but wouldn't give into the pressures and continued to develop the market up north. Why? "In business, one has to be fearless and do what one's inner voice tells you is the right thing," she says. "This has always given me inner-strength to stand up to anyone who would venture to impede my beliefs between what is right and what is unjust."

Devon Brooks, co-founder of the unique women's personal care business Blo Blow Dry Bars, knows a thing or two about fear. She was violently assaulted in two entirely separate incidents at 18 and 21 and went through the ensuing judicial process that eventually led to a guilty plea by both men. Summoning all her courage she made a personal commitment that she would never let her past get in the way of taking action.

Whether it was the fear of speaking in front of a few thousand people or meeting a new client, she always stops, reflects and then calls upon the strength that got her through before and then meets the challenge head on. Devon says, "Sometimes you live life, and sometimes life happens to you. But you always get to choose what you do about it."

Tim Clark of Business Model You adds an interesting perspective, "There is an entire industry of cheer-leading self-helpers who advocate you to do it, to make the jump and I will show you how to make it."

Tim believes that entrepreneurship isn't based on an idea or a plan, or even a model – it is based on having a strong competency in something. The way to overcome fear, he claims, is by testing your competency.

THE WORST POSSIBLE SCENARIO?

When fear raises its head in business decisions, Patrick McKeown finds it helpful to take a pen and paper and write down three possible scenarios.

- What is the best possible outcome?
- What is the worst possible outcome?
- What outcome falls between the above two?

Patrick says entrepreneurs who survive in the long term take calculated risks and tend not to take monumental courses of action with their head stuck in the sand.

FLOW FLOORS FEAR

For a group of Xceptionalists from Brazil, WeDemand.com, fear was never an issue. They have been so immersed in an industry they love, they haven't had the time or the inclination to be afraid. "I would tell entrepreneurs not to be afraid. If you sit around and just wish about your idea, nothing will happen. All you can lose is money and there is no shame in trying," says co-founder Bruno Natal. So, in essence, there is nothing to fear.

In my own career, apart from Melbourne, fear hasn't featured very often. I have always had an unshakable belief in my mission and as a result mastered the art of being comfortable in the uncomfortable. On a personal level, I have always had a fear of heights. However, the only way I knew how to deal with it was by facing and flooring it. Whenever our family would go to an adventure center, the first challenge I set myself was always the high ropes. Interestingly I would sweat the small and big stuff as I traveled those ropes but the feeling of exhilaration afterward definitely justified the effort. Over time the fear has reduced bit by bit. It's still there, but manageable.

It's ironic that one of most people's greatest fears is standing up in front of a group of people. Without doubt though that is my passion. While speaking I'm in flow and fear leaves the stage. The challenge for you, the entrepreneur, is to find your passion and make fear history.

4
EXPERT STATUS: STUDENT ALWAYS

THE ART OF RECIPROCATION

In 1998 I found myself on a plane heading towards the Andes in Peru. A teacher from Colorado I met along the way shared the following story about the importance of interdependence and the journey of going from 'I' to 'We'.

"When two indigenous Quechuans meet sixteen thousand feet atop a mountain in Peru for the first time, often they set a challenge. Let's say the challenge is a race. In their society, whoever wins the race is duty bound to coach the loser until he has attained a similar competency. In return, the loser teaches the victor a new skill. This interdependence helps both people. Both win, as does society. Ayni, the art of reciprocation, ensures that their society as a whole grows together."

What a beautiful way to live. Over time, I too have come to believe that a sense of interdependence is the final stage in our development as individuals.

The Quechuans acknowledge that we all have talents, and everyone is a potential teacher. It had a profound effect on me. This belief has single-handedly transformed my international fortunes so much that I now know that even the most annoying person could indeed be there to teach me something. To truly believe, you must move from the 'I' to 'We' paradigm.

You will find that there are zero degrees of separation from potential teachers. When you, the student, are ready, teachers will appear. The trick is that the teacher may just be the student. Do you believe that anybody could be your teacher?

SERENDIPITY

A former student of mine called wondering if I could help her brother Michael Heraghty, who was penning his first publication. A few days later we met. At the end, he asked how he could help as a 'thank you' for my time and ideas. He was a website designer and was happy to return the favor. Up until that point, few had dared surf onto my humble website, so this occupation didn't inspire much confidence in me. He persisted in his offer and I finally conceded. It transpired that he wasn't just any website designer.

Michael had worked on high profile online projects including Warner Music and one of the first online magazines in Ireland 'The Buzz'. He led the design team for one of the first European online banks IF.com. At zero cost to me, Michael designed a website that has consistently maintained a page one search engine ranking in many key phrases. The result of this has been a dramatic increase in enquiries and speaking engagements around the globe. So who was the student? And who was the teacher?

The student had become the teacher.

Businesses need to clearly embrace this philosophy, starting with their employees and customers.

Iza Login from Outfit7 illustrates its effectiveness, "When we started working with Disney on our first music video last March, they sent us the first song and Samo and I liked it. We then sent it out to all employees to hear their opinion. The feedback was everything else but positive. Then one of our new employees wrote an email to Samo highlighting how shocked he was that our testers and developers dared to express a negative opinion. Based on the feedback, we wrote to Disney to change the song and the final product was the fourth most watched video on YouTube in 2012. It pays to listen."

SELL THEM BACK THEIR PRODUCT

I am frequently asked to outline the strategies underpinning breaking sales records. One of these is to sell the customer back their product. Their product? Yes. In most of the companies where I've worked, either directly or as a consultant, one of the first steps was to speak to a representative sample of customers.

Part of the research brief would include seeking out potential improvements. Where possible, I would then investigate which of the customers' opinions were viable. Then, I would return to the target group and sell them our product plus their proposed revisions. The odds of a customer refusing their own product is smaller than when presenting your product.

By listening to his customers, Peldi from Balsamiq unleashed the businesses potential. He says, "I am definitely learning loads from the University of the Customer, the Coworker and the Community. At the outset our idea was to sell the mockup as a Confluence plugin. There was no intention of selling a desktop app. The reason behind this was that I was a one-man show, and I knew I couldn't maintain the necessary level of service required to develop it. However, my customers came on the site and pretty much demanded it. I had a rethink. Today 80% of our business is for desktop applications."

Oftentimes Balsamiq's meteoric rise has been judged as an overnight success, until you learn another part of the breakthrough story.

Peldi got his first computer book *How to Learn Basic* at around 12 years of age and is a self-professed life long student. "My major goal in business was to learn. I had legislated in my mind for failure. I had set aside a year's wages so I knew the worst possible scenario was I would learn a lot regardless of the outcome. This goal was the foundation for success of the business."

EXPERT STATUS

A commitment to ongoing learning is paramount in developing a world class xceptional business. From the word go, you must commit to becoming the expert in your field. Research conducted by Richard Boyatzis at Case Western Reserve University highlights the importance of learning in business. He found that the two skills linked to revenue generation and profitability were 'values learning' and 'facilitates learning'. The study involved a sample of about 1,300 partners in a financial consulting firm, out of which a sub-sample of 32 outstanding partners was identified using nominations from their subordinates, peers and their boss.

K. Anders Ericsson from Florida University, in his paper *The Making of an Expert*, claims it takes ten years to achieve expertise or 10,000 hours. He argues that experts are not born, they are made and, with what he describes as deliberate practice, you can develop expert status.

Guibert Englebienne, co-founder of Globant, is clear about the strategy underpinning their success. "The vision has been transformed as we journeyed. While we started by taking advantage of a window of opportunity of a cost advantage, we knew we couldn't survive in the long term unless we moved into being a premium provider.

Now the work we do is no longer a consequence of where we are from but of the expertise we've built that is hard to match. The focus is now on creating an agile, adaptive company. Without continually reinventing yourself you wouldn't be growing at this pace. We were a very confident group of people who grew even more confident with execution."

The strategy of continuous reinvention is only possible in a learning culture. Now, thanks to the digital revolution, you can tap into the latest information in your field at zero to minimal cost: Coursera, Khan Academy, Lynda, TED talks, Udacity, and Udemy to name a few.

Becoming an expert in your field no longer requires a massive budget. With expert status comes great confidence and great belief that you have something significant to share with your audience. You are ready for that next step. Willingness to learn is important, and willingness to act on what you learn is critical.

5
SEE YOURSELF

In 2007, the Stanford Business School Advisory Committee asserted that self awareness was the most important attribute a leader should develop. The promoter shapes and defines the culture. Self awareness is a pre-cursor for enhanced presence and the creation of an empowering culture. How aware are you?

SEE, THEN SOLVE

A father and son are involved in a tragic car accident. The father dies at the scene. The little boy is rushed to the emergency room at the hospital. On arrival, the doctor looks at the boy and exclaims, "This is my son." The question is – who is the doctor? Do you need to read it again? Confused? Don't worry you aren't the first person to feel that way. The answer of course is 'the mother'. I say 'of course' but I was one of the 50 percent who didn't get the answer right the first time around.

What happened? Deep in my subconscious I logged doctor = male, even though I have many doctor friends who are female. With that strongly held belief, I blocked out anything that contradicted my version of reality. I couldn't see the problem – something which is very common in business circles and in life.

Until you see and acknowledge this pattern, you can't solve it.

Over the past 25 years as a consultant, one thing I know for sure – it would have been a grave error to only seek the CEO or owner's point of view when assessing the prospects of a company. In the majority of cases, their opinion was far removed from what I was getting from employees or the marketplace.

Numerous studies highlight the gaps between leaders' perceptions of reality and insights on the ground. Some companies believe they are providing a good service, but customers don't concur. A study by Avaya showed that 80 percent of companies believed they were providing a quality service, to which only 8 percent of customers agreed. Leaders think they are doing a good job, but followers aren't following. Managers are happy that their team is engaged, but team members feel disconnected.

It gets worse. An intimate correlation exists between your physiology and your psychology. If you want a print out of a person's thinking, open your eyes. Who you are currently is obvious to others. You may not see it, but your customers and coworkers do. Research from Harvard psychology professors Ambady and Rosenthal confirms that people can make accurate assessments within seconds. From watching short silent videos of a professor in action in 10, 5 and 2 seconds clips, students were able to rate him on 15 different criteria, such as confidence, energy and warmth. Their scores tallied with how they assessed him at the end of the semester.

The analysis is over within seconds, but its findings could last a lifetime. The time you've got to make an impact is reducing and you have to make it count. You have got to know what version you are projecting to your customers. The challenge is it's like a virus. People aren't seeing situations as they are so problems remained unsolved. How do you eliminate this virus?

SEARCH INSIDE

A learned Indian teacher appeared in the sacred city of Varanasi, India, to show me the way. I was sitting against my rucksack in the railway station waiting for the next train.

Before he revealed his secret to life, two rats scurried behind my backpack. My self-protection senses were aroused, but the normal response of alarm bells going off in my system just didn't happen. I had been traveling now for six weeks in this magical country. I couldn't but reflect at that moment on how easy it is to become comfortable with the uncomfortable over time.

According to Indian folklore, he suggested, the Gods were discussing where to hide the secret of life so men and women would not find it.

"Hide it under a mountain," one God suggested.

"No," the Others disagreed. "One day they will find a way to dig up the mountain and uncover the secret of life."

"Put it at the bottom of the deepest ocean," another God

suggested. "It will be safe there."

"No," said the Others. "Someday people will find a way to travel to the bottom of the ocean and find it."

"Put it inside them," said the Third.

"Why?" asked the Others. "Because men and women will never think of looking for it there."

All agreed, and so it is said that the secret of life is hidden within us. What is the secret? It's discovering that special individual talent we all possess to unlock our true potential.

More immediately it is finding the years of programming lodged in your subconscious (or other than conscious mind) that could be holding you back.

Fear is learned, so you need to unlearn it. The first step is to find its source.

For Iza and Samo Login of Outfit7, it is simple, "If the entrepreneur is afraid, they suggest he/she needs to go away and reflect on the fear and highlight the blockages and negative beliefs in the subconscious underpinning it. On identification it is possible to face them and move on."

Your subconscious is a storage facility for your attitudes and beliefs about life, your life's metaphors, both positive and negative, and acts similar to a computer. Like any computer if you continue to input garbage, all you can expect output wise is indeed garbage. You need to ensure that you have the best virus protection to avoid hacking. If your daily diet is one of doom and gloom, and this is what you are presenting for input, it is hard to see how an optimistic, positive entrepreneur would be the by-product of this program.

SICKURITY

Many people at a very young age were brainwashed to focus on the permanent and pensionable. In other words get married, settle down and have the 2.1 kids and live happily ever after, promoting the secure path as opposed to the risky entrepreneurial life. It promotes 'security' thinking – or in my mind, 'sickurity'.

I was brought up in a very entrepreneurial setting and my parents, with love, advised me to take the safer route. I diverged, realizing that 'here today, gone today, live life now' was for me the only way. Because of my awareness, I was able to choose differently. To help unearth these patterns, the entrepreneur should at minimum sit down and reflect on the major influences in their life and what they integrated from them.

This is not a blame game, it is a pattern identification exercise. In addition it would be useful to reflect on the major events in your life to date and see how they shaped you. It was fascinating interviewing the Xceptionalists and finding a mixture emerging of positive parental influence and dysfunction in the context of developing them into the business people they are today.

One of the tools that can help unearth your subconscious truths is learning how to calm your mind. The ability to quieten and still your noisy overactive mind can help in highlighting and eliminating viruses as well as enhancing your creativity, clarity and decision-making.

Studying with the Quechuan people in Peru in 1996, I got my first lesson in doing nothing. The trip had been an eye opener to put it mildly. Here in the undeveloped world, I was learning many developed ideas. The native people argued that westerners live on the left side: We are always busy and never have time. In contrast, they have infinite time on the right side. They enjoy doing nothing. Time passes us by, but they pass through time.

I was instructed to find a place and sit in silence for two hours. High up in the Andes and surrounded by the most breathtaking scenery, I can remember sitting there questioning my idleness. My mind was buzzing. 'When is something going to happen?' I wondered. 'I didn't come all the way across the world to learn nothing. I haven't got the time. What's the point of doing nothing? What am I learning?'

The quieter I became physically, the louder and louder my mind appeared to be. 'Is this nothingness the catalyst for insanity?' I mused. This inner noise had always been there, and the only difference now was that I was listening.

My teacher's instruction was clear and simple. Listen and acknowledge the noise, then re-focus. Once every thought was acknowledged, it allowed me to return my focus to the beautiful scenery. Acknowledge and refocus. Over time the gap between my thoughts started to widen, and the noise began to subside, little by little.

During my time there, I took many time-outs, cradled up in the breathtaking Andes. Initially the exercise was a challenge. Over time it was the tonic for an out of sync mind. Now, whenever I feel stressed, lacking energy, experiencing writer's block or am unclear in my decision-making, I go down to the sea and focus on the movement or the sound of the waves. Thoughts pop into my head, but after acknowledging them, my focus returns to the waves. Within minutes the knots start to unravel.

"THE OCEAN DISENTANGLES THE NETTED MIND." – ANONYMOUS

I wasn't the first to discover the power of switching off. The Xceptionalists have been on the case for some time.

Patrick McKeown, CEO of Asthma Care, in his own words would have gone mad if he hadn't learned how to tame his internal chatter. "I experienced many moments of doubt during my early days. On many occasions questions like 'Am I crazy doing this?' and 'What happens if it doesn't succeed?' popped into my mind. Thankfully I found relief from the very therapy I was teaching. By focusing attention on my breath, I was able to switch off a very busy mind and, after a few minutes, ready to refocus on the task at hand. Without learning this exercise, I would be out of business and a mental wreck. So, very simply on a number of occasions througout the day, regardless of whether my day was fantastic or disappointing, I would take a few minutes timeout at my desk and focus on the flow of my breath. Any stray negative or positive thoughts were acknowledged and followed by returning my focus to the breath. It reduced the traffic in my mind and allowed me to see things more clearly and be creative."

Agnes McCourt of Unislim says, "To switch off, my daily routine includes an early morning meditation for 15 minutes. This tends to be followed by some light exercise before I go down the stairs and have my breakfast. Golf, swimming and crosswords all help me to still and clear the mind – an essential part of my life that helps me make better decisions and sharpen the sixth sense, my intuition which is an important adviser."

Devon Brooks of Blo Blow Dry Bar echoes this too, "For me outdoors is my escape. Nature saves me, nature nourishes me – it keeps me sane. Every single day I take time out to indulge in nature. My fiancé and I 'take it to the trees' for every important life decision. One thing I have realized is that no matter what avenues I pursue in the future, time for nature will be a non-negotiable part of the routine, if not a part of the master plan."

Academics also concur. Jon Kabat-Zinn and neuroscientist Richard Davidson of the University of Wisconsin found that after eight weeks of mindfulness-based stress reduction a group of biotech employees showed a greater increase in activity in the left prefrontal cortex – the region of the brain associated with a happier state of mind, optimism and resilience – than colleagues who received no training. Happiness correlates to increased productivity, enhanced presence, idea generation and more.

You don't need to be in absolute silence to allow your thoughts and ideas to surface. The mild buzz of a coffee shop can get your thoughts flowing as well. Yes, those people who populate coffee shops around the world aren't all unproductive workers. I know, because a lot of this book was written in my local coffeehouse.

University of British Columbia researchers asked over 300 participants to work on creative tasks in nearly silent, moderately loud (70 decibels, or about what you would expect in a coffee shop) and very loud environments. Results published in the Journal of Consumer Research showed that a moderate (70 dB) versus low (50 dB) level of noise enhanced the flow of creativity, while a high level of noise (85 dB) damages it. Indeed you don't even have to go to the coffee shop any more – you can recreate that experience online.

With a calm mind comes self-awareness, allowing you to unearth limiting patterns and then choose to disempower them. With practice, pushing yourself a little further each time, you can replace limiting beliefs with patterns of a more empowering nature.

6
ROI: RETURN ON INTUITION

Have you ever met someone, maybe a supplier or potential business partner, where your immediate reaction was negative? Maybe it was a feeling about a certain project? You got a bad feeling but dismissed this information to your peril.

You're not alone. Based on reactions from audiences from around the world, I can certainly say that a lot of people aren't using the most powerful tool in their business locker - their gut. Your intuition is a refined source of insight, a compass for your entrepreneurial journey.

All my life, my focus, my compass, has been my intuition. A knowing without the knowledge, a feeling and an instinct, guiding impulses to which I paid attention and provided clarity in the dark.

Early 1996, my intuition was promoting an ambitious dream – to write a bestselling personal excellence book. Ambitious it was, but it felt right so I dared to dream. To start the process, I printed 'I am a Best Selling author' and 'Manuscript finished by May 28th', then placed the A4 sheets on the back of my office door and over my workspace. The idea was to imprint a desired reality on my subconscious – in simpler terms, there was no getting away from the dream.

My friends and business colleagues highlighted obvious obstacles that lay ahead. English was not my strongest subject. In my final school examination, I earned a poor 'D' grade. I was consistent and also got a 'D' in my junior exam. Writing and speaking are two very different disciplines, and I had no experience of writing. You may ask how did I pick May 28th? It felt right!

Famous American writers predominantly controlled the self-help market so I was being very optimistic to believe their stranglehold could be broken. Indeed, three very close business confidantes told me unanimously that I had no chance of writing a bestselling book. There was also a view that I was too young to be taken seriously. We didn't even discuss how I was going to find a publisher or motivate people to buy my book.

It's fair to say that the prevailing opinion was against my adventure, but with trust in my heart, I swam against this considerable tide to honor my inner whispers. George Bernard Shaw was my inspiration. "You see things; and you say, 'Why?' But I dream things that never were; and I say, 'Why not?'"

My focus remained on the dream, believing the map would appear in time. Within a few weeks there was a knock on my door from a lady from the local area with whom I'd exchanged pleasantries in the past. She heard I was writing a book and wondered if she could help. It transpired that Margaret was a retired English teacher and poet. Considering my erratic academic past, she was just the person I needed on the team. My learning mindset said that she could be my teacher.

A few weeks later, I was invited to keynote at the Network Women in Business National Conference. Afterwards, the president of the organization committed to publishing my book. Then more people turned up who contributed to the core content until, on May 28th, the manuscript was finished. To be precise, my last edit happened on May 27th.

I continued focusing on my dream to convert it into reality. Every town I visited, I called to bookshops to merchandise and sign books. Publicity was initiated in all my target regions. How? When You Don't Know How became a bestseller and I was beside myself with happiness.

Intuition plus execution is a powerful cocktail. Many entrepreneurs share my contention that it can have a dramatic effect on your bottom line. You certainly can expect an ROI, a return on intuition.

Ben Milne of Dwolla says, "I have had many times where I didn't go against the logical argument put in front of me even though it didn't feel right. It came back to bite me in the ass. I know the first impression thing is a bit clichéd but if you have a bad feeling about someone or a deal, go with the feeling. Otherwise it amplifies over time. By overthinking and trying to justify it, it only gets worse."

Tim Clark from Business Model You adds, "You have to trust your gut. The challenge is people trust their gut less and less with all the analytical tools at their disposal. For me, many of my biggest decisions relied on my gut feeling. When I decided to move to Japan, many thought I didn't know what I was doing. For me, at a deeper level, I was totally confident in the decision. It felt right. While there, I started a Japanese internet company, which was the result of an informed intuitive understanding.

This company was sold onto China.com in a multi-million dollar deal. When Alex Osterwalder was building the Business Generation Model, I was the 20th person to sign up to help in the venture. Very early on they advertized for an editor. Immediately, I applied and indicated that I was the right man for the job and was willing to do it for nothing. I didn't logically know where this was going but my gut did. This was to be a pivotal moment in my career."

Intuition is the entrepreneur's tool that gives direction and clarity at all times if you listen to it. And psychological research is bearing its effectiveness out.

Even as far back as 1994, a survey by Jagdish Parikh, a Harvard Business School student, showed that of 1300 managers from nine nations the respondents indicated that they used their intuitive skills as much as they used their analytical abilities, but they credited 80 percent of their successes to instinct.

A more recent global survey of 368 start-ups carried out by Geckoboard and Econsultancy in February 2013 also highlighted that intuition is still very much valued with only 27 percent of respondents believing that data is crucial when it comes to decision-making.

7
CRACKING THE CODE

341005003056555641289

Your challenge, should you choose to accept it, is to crack the above code. If successful, you're on the way to unlocking the secret to loyalty and engagement. Any ideas? This figure, a combination of results from different research studies, pretty much sums up how difficult it is to get your message across.

We are exposed to 34 gigabytes of information and 100,500 words daily, according to How much information? 2009 Report on American Consumers conducted by the Global Information Industry Center of the University of California, San Diego. On average every three minutes and five seconds you are interrupted from your task at hand says Gloria Mark, Professor in the Department of Informatics at the University of California at Irvine, in her work *Interuption*.

Attention deficit is no longer the supposed domain of Generation Y, who were brought up on a diet of social media and new technology. A recent study by IBM revealed 65 percent of 55-64 year olds surf, text and watch television simultaneously.

The average attention span in 2012 was 8 seconds, which is down significantly from 2000 when it was 12 seconds, according to statistics published in the Associated Press, comparing it with that of a gold fish which is 9 seconds. In an 24/7 always-on world, inundated with advertising and social media, smartphone pings and text messages, distraction is the new normal.

Presentation has replaced conversation and monologue trumps dialogue. Winning a friendly and authentic ear is a rare experience. Therein lies the opportunity.

Tim Clark, founder of Business Model You, sums it up: "There's a reason. It's called 'paying" attention'! It's a substantial cost in terms of time and energy. But nothing fundamental has changed. Everyone is still amazed when you actually listen deeply to what they are saying and respond to that rather than simply waiting them out so you can spew forth your own points."

Entrepreneurs who develop an xceptional mindset shower their customers and co-workers with quality authentic attention – the most sought after intangible in an attention deficit society.

The DGAs, 'Do Give Attention' people, have the potential to achieve cult status, as I appeared to achieve with a very difficult participant at one of my speaking engagements many years ago.

10 BILLION BRAIN CELLS BUT EVERYONE'S A CHRISTY

I was commissioned to do a keynote with a group of 50 people who worked for a multinational company. Before I was introduced, a man shouted out from the back of the group, "When is this going to be over?"

'Not a great start', I thought. Since his interjection had raised a question in everyone's mind, I began by reassuring the audience that my input would be brief. I then addressed my impatient friend, requesting his name.

"Christy," he said.

"Christy, imagine that you are interviewing me for a sales job. I want you and the audience to assess me before I even open my mouth. Please analyze how I walk into the interview room, how confident is my handshake and so on."

I walked down to the back of the room and gave him a strong, confident handshake and went back to the podium.

"Ok," I said, addressing the whole room, "Just remember that Christy is interviewing me for a sales job. His task – and yours – is to record your first impressions."

I walked back to him again and shook his hand again before returning to the podium. After the third time, I requested his feedback, which was mentally recorded. A few minutes later, directing my attention away from him, I said, "As Christy mentioned earlier," and repeated the most relevant comment he had made.

By now there was a major shift in his body language. He was sitting forward with his eyes firmly fixed on me. He had moved from being a big challenge in the learning environment to, at the very least, being neutral. What happened?

Christy had delivered a high-powered learning experience. He had articulated a basic need that many would shy away from declaring consciously but nonetheless demand. Christy wanted quality attention, like any customer or co-worker does. Execution must be underpinned by this understanding to truly engage.

I knew that if I delivered quality attention, there would be a dramatic change in his attitude, delivered in different ways.

INCLUSION

Christy was made to feel wanted by including him in the exercise. Clearly he is more likely to be engaged if he is part of the show. Asking questions and including people in the conversation should be the base level strategy for any persuader. Be warned that when you ask, allow people the opportunity to respond. Too often honoring an insatiable appetite for attention, people look like they are going to pounce on their colleagues as they wait to either interrupt or 'present' their contribution.

NAME PLEASE

Most people love to hear their own name, but use it sparingly, particularly if you don't know the person, otherwise it will be perceived as a gimmick.

THE POWER OF TOUCH

The handshake helps to establish connection and build rapport. Studies have shown that touching someone on the upper arm for just a second or two can have a significant effect on how much help they will provide. In Gueguen's 2007 study researchers approached people on the street asking for a dime – the touch increased the possibility of cash by 20 percent. A study from the Touch Institute at the University of Miami showed that a little touch on the shoulder was enough to make people tell the truth and return the money they had found in a phone booth.

REPETITION

Another great rapport builder is repeating back to people what they have said, demonstrating not only the ability to listen, but you are also attaching importance to the words.

When I, the perceived expert in this situation, referred the audience to Christy's comments, I validated his input helping him to feel very good about himself. Some years back the lead singer of The Corrs, an Irish band, described their reaction to the crowd singing their songs back to them as the equivalent of a spiritual experience. In negotiations I believe repetition of key points has the same effect.

For a study from the University of Nijmegen a waitress was asked to request orders from the customers in two ways: (1) Listen and be generally positive and polite. (2) Repeat the order back to the customer. The second method resulted in 70 percent larger tips than from those in the first group. As an aside, what if customer service personnel repeated back to clients, in a retail setting, their order? Would it increase the possibility of a more lucrative order?

SPOTLIGHT ON THE CUSTOMER

What happens when trainers move around a room? Usually the audience follows them with their eyes. Each time I went over to Christy everyone else was feeding him attention at a subconscious level and he reveled in it. People tell me that this is a source of embarrassment. But it is only their conscious response, which isn't aligned with their subconscious truth. We are inside out, not outside in. Always remember there is a Christy in every room.

How do you put the delivery of quality attention to your customers at the forefront of your execution strategy? It starts with an innovative and essential business strategy. You need to focus on building friendships, not customer relationships.

People crave genuine, authentic, undivided attention, the side effect of which is extremely positive: loyalty, engagement and positive word-of-mouth promotion.

8
CHOOSE FRIENDS OVER CUSTOMERS

The case for friendships? It's simply the only sustainable strategy available. When people are asked who they most trust to recommend a product or service the answer is consistently 'someone like me'. Peers are perceived to be more credible and informed than sales personnel. Meanwhile the business reality is clear – customers leave, friends don't. Even satisfied customers leave. The customer as a concept in its current interpretation is dead. If you are dealing with the client as a customer, your business may be in trouble. When they become your friend in its true sense, you have them for life.

The power of friendships helped Globant built their world-class business. When they committed to starting a company, their first exercise was to write down all their friends and contacts. Then, with a developed sales presentation and a $5,000 start-up budget, they sat down with them in different parts of the globe and ended up identifying many opportunities.

Ben Milne from Dwolla accentuates this, "The biggest deals without doubt are based on relationships. Granted, where someone is buying a book or some software which is a 30 second decision, you don't have that rapport, but for the bigger decisions that have wider implications, it is down to whether you like a person or not. If it is the latter, you won't recruit or buy from them."

The same logic applies with respect to building relationships within your team. Friendships in the workplace will also have a positive effect on the bottom line. Gallup research has shown that employees who have best friends at work are seven times more likely to be engaged in their job.

In WeDemand friendships are the strong foundation on which they are building their business. according to co-founder Bruno Natal, "Four of the five co-founders know each other from their college days when we either locked horns on the football pitch or collaborated on a literature fanzine. The final director, Pedro, became friendly with me when I was completing my Masters in Documentary Film Making in London in 2007. I invited him on board. Most of us know each other for 15 years. It is now like a marriage. We all know our boundaries, our strengths and weaknesses. We know what buttons not to push and what road not to travel on in the context of working with each other. The relationship has changed because of course we now have a very new baby but our friendships see us through most scenarios."

Interestingly WeDemand's original offering potentially allowed customers to get to see their favorite band for free if the gig was successful. After extensive research of over 6,000 clients, they found that being involved in organizing a concert in their home city was the motivator, not the financial rewards that accrued if it sold out. In summary significance trumped cash.

Friendships are built on trust. People enjoy and more importantly trust real people and can see when someone is playing a game. A culture of trust starts at the top. Authentic leadership is a precursor for creating sustainable relationships. If you are committed to this, people will pick up on it from your presence quicker than you can imagine.

"We're finding that everything is evaluated as good or bad within a quarter of a second," says John A. Bargh, highlighting one undisputable fact: The majority of people are getting an exact printout of who you are within seconds. To build a high trust culture, you need to project a trustworthy presence.

DO DIFFERENT

To build friendships, you need a new selling philosophy. Traditionally the focus in sales was merely transactional. You bought, I sold, money was exchanged – deal done. The new approach means that the main work begins after the deal is done.

POSE THE QUESTIONS

- When did I last secure business for my client?
- Could I suggest different product ideas for their mix?
- Could I send through competitor information?
- How can I give even more for less?

Motivate everyone to be a sales person. In Africa they say it takes a village to raise a child. In business, it takes everyone to sell the business. Thus, adopting best practice from such companies as Zappos, Dyson and many others, all staff should have an intimate knowledge of the customer service strategies and/or the production process. Everybody who joins Dyson makes a vacuum cleaner on their first day and then takes it home so they own one. Similarly every employee should know what business you're in and communicate that in a meaningful way.

HEALTHY PARANOIA

Paranoia is acceptable in the new friendship paradigm. Worrying that your best employees or customers might leave is okay, as long as you put in place an active strategy to offset any possibility of that scenario.

Forensically examine every point of contact between your customers and the organization and focus on exceeding expectations at every opportunity. For instance, how quickly are people dealt with when they walk into the reception area or what is the accepted lead time between a telephone enquiry and the delivery of promotional information and materials?

Quick test – while reading the following story, try to determine the type of business described:

The gold plated sign outside the door says 'by appointment only'. As the door is locked, there is no opportunity for walk-ins.

You must be either an existing customer or referred by another client to gain entry. When the door opens, your eyes are guided towards a big cappuccino machine and your senses are heightened by the smell of freshly baked cupcakes.

The attendee greets you by name and you are brought to a private lounge where you can relax on the comfortable sofas and enjoy some tea from a set of very expensive china. The lounge is opulently decorated, smelling and looking differently to any direct competitor. Where are you?

After a few minutes, a knock on the door. It is the dentist to discuss your needs. Yes, you are visiting the dental practice of Paddi Lund in Australia. After the consultation you make the short walk down the corridor, at the end of which is a beautiful mural.

This is a fantastic example of an organization that is managing many of the contact points with the customer. What is the smell you most associate with a dental practice? Certainly not coffee and baking. More likely it is antiseptic which drives the cortisol levels even higher.

Paddi explains the strategy underlying his xceptional service, "I have reviewed all the good experiences I have had in church, shopping and in restaurants and considered how they could be integrated into the environment I offer my customers. If we can change the atmosphere, we change the client's mindset and we control the experience. It is a little like taking someone to the theater. If I can open my client's mind to a different point of view, I have a greater chance that they will be receptive to treatments they are not familiar with. If I am able to show my customer amazing attention to detail in the hospitality I offer, they are more likely to believe I will show the same care and attention to their comfort during treatment. And if I can help my customers to relax, clinical dentistry is easier for us both."

There is always room for improvement. Your focus should be on delivering that little bit extra. That may be the hot towel I got when booking into the Hotel Jumeriah on Central Park after a long transatlantic flight or how a local personality was approached by staff as she left the Lane Crawford building in Hong Kong with her favourite lemon cake on the occasion of her birthday. The point is that little bit extra can make a big difference.

CELEBRATING COMPLAINTS

One key contact point that companies struggle with is complaints handling. Instead of celebrating them, they are avoided like the plague. A complaint is a unique opportunity to strengthen the relationship with the client. The fact is that most people don't expect them to be dealt well, so when you train your team to detonate this potential time bomb at base, you immediately exceed expectations.

Celebrating a lack of complaints is like celebrating a movement towards bankruptcy. Remember, 96 percent of dissatisfied people never complain to you directly but leave anyway, according to Technical Assistance Research Program, USA. Complacency allows you to listen to complaints – paranoia demands you ask, then solve and move the customer closer to being a friend.

Some time ago I purchased a pair of shoes. Two days later, the shoes were making their debut in the auspicious surroundings of the Grimaldi Forum in Monaco. Just before being introduced to the audience, the sole of one of the shoes detached itself. Never one to take myself too seriously, I turned the crisis into a comedy and addressed the audience in my socks.

When I got home, I revisited the shop, approached the customer service staff and explained the situation. After reviewing the shoes and the receipt, she indicated that she would have to speak with the manager. I was left standing at the top of a growing line of impatient shoppers while she discussed my case with her superior before eventually refunding my money.

Impressed? I wasn't. The only acceptable way of dealing with that situation would have been an sincere apology followed by a refund on the spot. Nobody needs a further cross-examination or an induced feeling of guilt as your case is thrashed out in front of other customers. They lost the opportunity to move me along the continuum from customer to friend.

Based on the following research from Harris, it appears that our complaints handling online is even worse. 42 percent expect a response within a day, yet only 22 percent got one. Meanwhile 98 percent of respondents have taken action as a result of a negative experience and 79 percent have told others about it. The message is clear whether online or off. If you want to develop friendships, you need to improve your ability to deal with complaints.

If you want to go one step further, design a customer charter with your team that guarantees the levels of service your customer can expect at each contact point. This takes away the risk of buying from you and sends a very clear message to the market: You have total confidence in your product or service and the people who deliver it.

RECRUIT RIGHT

Culture is king and recruitment is key in maintaining and enhancing it. Your strategy should focus on attracting those with the right attitude, not just current ability. If you are looking to build friendships with your customers, you need warm, friendly, authentic and fun front line staff. People often preach the need for experience or expertise in the chosen field. Give me a person with energy and enthusiasm any day.

Many years ago, I recruited someone for the post of trainer and administrative manager for my own company even though, on paper, she wasn't qualified. She had scraped through her final school exams and her sole expertise was in typesetting. However, at the interview she proved to be a very good listener and was clearly willing to learn. My instinct told me that she could make the leap from being a typesetter to speaking in front of the most demanding audience in the world – teenagers. After immersing herself in the content for about six months, she got her first opportunity. She was an instant hit.

Have you got an eye for the right candidate? Many companies recruit around their values or, at minimum, hire someone they believe has the ability to adapt. Some of the Xceptionalists emphasized how their intuition played a major part in recruitment. In summary if it doesn't feel right, it is time to move on.

Iza Login from Outfit7, a personal development enthusiast, has her own way of attracting desired candidates. "We were looking for a person to take responsibility for our webstore. All applicants were somehow good but we always try to find an excellent candidate. When I went to bed, I thought, 'There should be someone perfect for our store. I would like to meet him or her.'

The next morning before awakening, I got the picture of a guy that worked for me as a student 10 years previously. He had really impressed me with his intelligence and managing skills and he was only 17 back then, but I couldn't remember his name. It took me at least 10 minutes to recall it. I then found him on LinkedIn, wrote him an email and we had the first call the same day.

A month later, he was a part of our team. He settled in and told me his story. His previous job wasn't challenging enough and he eventually fell into despair. He vowed to go to church every day for nine consecutive days and pray for guidance in discovering a new vocation. On the ninth day I emailed him. We both manifested which was preceded by a positive intention."

Guibert Englebienne from Globant continues, "When you find unique talent, recruit it. We are now always looking for people who fascinate us, know more about a subject than we do. The time is always right to recruit a person like that. Through our talent management systems we are always juggling around what is the best role for different people."

Ben Milne of Dwolla adds, "Recruit on creativity and aptitude was the advice given to me by the ex CTO of Best Buy, advice that has stuck with me to this day. There's no science in business. Just find good people and don't be an asshole.

The trick is to surround yourself with fantastic people you can trust, who can be your eyes and see things that you couldn't possibly see anyway. I surround myself with great people who act like bumpers in my life. From the conservative to the extreme, the mix helps to improve the decision-making. What's the point in employing smart people if you aren't going to listen to them? Yes, sometimes I think things could be done faster and better, but I also think of the need to get the best out of my people and the fact that overall our decision making is better."

9
DREAM IT

What if I told you one of the great obstacles to realizing your entrepreneurial dreams is that small voice inside that whispers: I am not good enough. Rewind your life and find compelling evidence that you have what it takes to excel. From the wisdom you showed as a child, to the unconscious strategy used when making significant decisions, to the flow you experience in the zone, you clearly have what it takes.

CHILDISH WISDOM

Every minute I spend with our little boy Conor reaffirms in me the belief that we are all pure potential, born with the xceptional execution gene. For the first five years of his life, he recorded many remarkable achievements with an underlying program worth benchmarking.

Within 18 months, he mastered the challenging act of walking. Within 5 years, he became proficient in a new language having acquired over 80 percent of the words necessary to communicate effectively. All this without the aid of a teacher. Not bad. Both were achieved through focus, learning from feedback, perseverance and boundless energy – all desirable and necessary attributes for the modern entrepreneur

In the case of Agnes McCourt, founder of Unislim, like many of the Xceptionalists, childlike perseverance helped her build her business. "I travelled through all the local estates door by door introducing our slimming classes idea. It wasn't the easiest sell.

At one doorstep the response was immediate and decisive. The woman nearly took the nose off me permanently. She smashed the door in my face and strangely has never spoken to me in the 40 years since. I was the third of nine children and was brought up with a strong work ethic. As my father had emphasized to all the family, 'God gave his bird the food but he didn't throw him the nest.'"

For Conor, just like many children, a box tends to be the catalyst for more fun than the enclosed toy. It can be a space ship, a slide, a home, a container, a mode of transport. The list is endless. With creativity clearly seen as a necessary prerequisite for success in the current market, it appears the child has that creative flair. And there is proof.

A Study of Genius by George Land and Beth Jarmin published in 1993 in their book *Breakpoint and Beyond* found that 98 percent of 2-5 year olds, 32 percent of all 8-10 year olds, and 10 percent of all 13-15 year olds from the group of 1,600 children tested were in the creative genius category. Of 200,000 adults surveyed, just 2 percent of those over 25 could be considered creative geniuses. The magic doesn't have to stop when you pass childhood.

MAGNETIC ATTRACTION

Every day you experience special moments, sometimes outside your conscious attention. Did you notice that when pursuing a goal, you appear to have a natural ability to attract the support and information necessary for success. For example when buying a car, moving house or locating a business premises? Due to its importance a significant amount of time and energy is invested in the process.

When you think about anything at length it moves from your conscious to your subconscious mind. You actually create new neural pathways in the brain. The more you think about something, the stronger the connections grow and the more deeply ingrained the thought becomes.

Your subconscious has an efficient filtering system that will help you see what you want to see and attract what you need to attract. For instance, as soon as you decide to change that car, a sequence of events appear to occur that prove you have this magnetic ability to attract the information you require.

Have you ever noticed how car dealerships suddenly seem to be everywhere, or that the local dealer premises had moved closer to the road. You couldn't but be drawn to it as you passed by? It looks like the media has got an inside scoop on your specific desires, because every time you pick up the paper it is full of car adverts. When you switch on the TV, a similar pattern emerges.

What's happening? You have set an important goal, one that

you are willing to focus on and invest some time and energy. The process of attracting teachers, circumstances and events then kicks in to help you achieve the desired outcome. After you bought the car, you start to see people driving the exact same model. No need to worry, you've made the right decision.

Peldi of Balsamiq agrees, "When I made the decision to leave Adobe and start up, I didn't sleep for four full nights beforehand. This was even considering that my move was in many ways the end of a one-year plan to be ready for takeoff. A year previous to that it appeared like a cosmic thing. Everything started falling into place to facilitate my big move.

Initially, my landlord in San Francisco informed us that he was selling the building in a year's time. It was a case of, 'buy the apartment for a $1 million or leave'. My mother contacted me and told me she was going to rent out the apartment that I grew up in or give it to me if I wanted to return. Then my boss quit in Adobe, giving me the chance over the next year to lead a small team – something I needed experience in and I knew would be invaluable in the context of my dream.

After that year, I would have reached the middle management ceiling. The next step was to move on. My son was 2 years old and we knew if all failed in Italy, we could return to the USA and get a job – no major problem. All this combined to facilitate the move back home and the launch of my new business."

PASSION ON PURPOSE

In the late 2000s, I was struck down with a mysterious virus. I was barely able to get out of bed and to the bathroom. Focusing on my computer screen for more than a minute was a task too far. The only problem was, I had a scheduled call with the Managing Director and Human Resources Manager of a multinational medical firm that afternoon. A potential assignment with all their Directors the following month in New York was on the table. Canceling the call wasn't an option.

Fifteen minutes before the call, I struggled into the office, flopped on the chair and tried to mentally prepare for the conference call. On cue, the phone rang. From the moment I answered, the illness seems to have lifted. We had a fantastic conversation. In the end the Managing Director commented on my remarkable abundance of energy and enthusiasm and awarded me the keynote.

I wasn't off the phone thirty seconds when I realized that the illness hadn't passed after all. I rang the doctor and secured an immediate appointment. She diagnosed Swine flu. Many people have had similar experiences where energy was always available when doing what they loved. Passion is truly found in purpose.

XCEPTIONAL OPPORTUNITY

We are all hardwired for success. The programming is in place. You just need to re-activate it. It can be used for all your personal and business goals, from attempts to develop your domestic market to developing an international presence.

Unlike any other time in history, it is now possible to tell the world about your great idea at minimal cost. To develop your idea, you can outsource many aspects at very competitive rates. You can recruit your own multinational team from your home office.

In my pursuits I partner with people around the world – a project manager in Australia, an editor in the USA, designers in England and Canada, web gurus in India, book printers in China and speaking agents from across the globe. The list continues.

There's no excuse to not dream big. You can dream the impossible of becoming the Starbucks of the hairdressing industry or eliminating credit cards from our pockets. You can take on any established industry, even with a few thousand dollars in your pocket, or start a business aimed at world domination without any idea of how you are going to do it.

The choice is yours. The process starts with intent, with a dream and the journey is the destination. Xceptional execution allows you to enjoy the magic.

10
DO IT

The clock is ticking. Stop waiting for that elusive and mythical 'aha' moment. Stop over-thinking and embrace a bias towards action – a bent towards doing. As Dwolla's Ben Milne put it, "Do it or don't. If you are going to, shut up and do it. The more you talk, the more you are missing the opportunity."

It's time to DO!

15 STRATEGIES FOR XCEPTIONAL EXECUTION

1. Sign your name

Commit to becoming an expert in your chosen field, or at minimum proficient at your current job as a precursor for the dream move. To start the process, sign your name on the dotted line.

....

2. Accept zero separation

Would you like to have access to the best people in the world? If so, take out a business card or open the notes section of your smartphone. Record the question: "Did I believe that everyone could be my teacher today?" Review this question daily for 30 days. After 30 days, it should become a habit. The more you open yourselves up to new teachers, the more you improve the odds of reaching your goals. One simple pattern can transform fortunes.

3. Activate your subconscious power

Consciously we are limited, but subconsciously unlimited. An exercise illustrates the point: With a pencil in each hand, draw a circle with your left hand and a circle with your right hand at the same time. Now draw a circle with your right hand and a square with your left hand simultaneously. It's okay to draw a square with your right hand and a circle with your left hand at the same time if you so wish. How did you get on? It is likely that the first task didn't stretch you too much. Why? Because I asked you to do one thing at any one time in your conscious mind, i.e. draw a circle with both hands. However, for most the second part of the exercise is not so easy because focusing consciously on two things simultaneously is not a runner. Yet at the subconscious level, multitasking is a given.

Random thoughts pop in and out of your mind no matter how engaged you are. These thoughts are arriving from your 'other than conscious' mind. New cells are being produced all the time, so it is fair to say that you are continuously recreating your body, again outside conscious control. Breathing works in the same way. You don't have to stop mid sentence and say to yourself, 'I will have another five hundred breaths please.'

What about autopilot? Was there ever an occasion in the past when, while driving long distance, you could not recall passing through some town or village along the way? No doubt about it. You have obviously been on autopilot. It appears that we also have a protection mechanism in our subconscious facility.

Processing power: Your subconscious has a strong processing facility. You can switch focus from the task at hand and your subconscious will work quietly in the background to execute.

In an experiment, Stephen Smith from Texas A & M University showed volunteers picture and word puzzles that suggested common phrases and asked them to solve as many as possible, such as 'You just me'. The answer is 'Just between you and me'. If unsuccessful in solving the puzzle, they were told to relax for 15 minutes and then try again. Amazingly, a third more problems were solved on the second attempt, because as they relaxed their subconscious worked on the solution.

4. Identify your core beliefs

- Life is ....
- I am ....
- What I want most is ....
- Failure is ....

What were your first reactions? There are no right or wrong answers, but here are a few empowering and not so empowering ones. 'Life's a bitch' was the answer from one of my course participants some years back. It surprised him, but not me. From early on, his physiology screamed discomfort, unease and more.

Though he continued to spin positively about life in public, his underlying metaphors were negative. For him this disclosure was the start of a great personal journey. He started seeing the pattern, now he could move on to the solution. A more empowering response would be 'life is a journey of magic and adventure.' Is that yours?

5. Analyze your actions

James Joyce said, "The actions of men are the best interpreters of their thoughts." Review your actions in life for a true insight into your thinking. This will help you identify your current thought process.

- Are you at least doing something practical about developing your business idea or are you still 'all talk'?
- Are you attracting positive, helpful people who will contribute to moving you closer to your goal or prophets of doom who drag you down?
- How is your language? Do you find yourself using self-deprecating words like 'should', 'can't', 'might', 'but', 'never', 'problem' or uplifting words such as 'will', 'can', 'always', or 'challenge'?
- How important are your people's ideas and beliefs? Are you paying lip service or have you created structures that allow employees the opportunity for training and development, a forum for them to express their opinions and ideas and give

constructive evaluation of their performance?

- Are you confident enough in your product or service to send customers off to the competition? If the thought strikes fear in your heart, you need a rethink.

6. Be your mind's guardian

Your mind works very similar to a personal computer – garbage in, garbage out. If you want to stay motivated and indeed be able to face and floor any doubts you have, it is necessary to become your mind's guardian. Monitor everything that is presented for entry into your personal software. Thousands of thoughts zip through your mind on a daily basis, normally 90 percent cent of those are the same as the previous day. You need to ensure that the majority of these are positive and empowering.

7. Intend intuitive execution

Intuition is potentially your best business app. It's free and ahead of the game. You need to reflect on how it delivers? Does it manifest as an inner voice, a vision or a feeling? Awareness is paramount. When you know how it delivers, you will have more confidence in executing its promptings. Your intuition works like a muscle; the more you use it, the stronger it gets.

8. Aim for zen living

If only you could see the wood for the trees? To make better decisions, you need to calm your mind and live in the now. Sit with your back straight, shoulders relaxed and chin slightly tucked in. Ensure that your knees are lower than your hips, and allow your hands to rest on your thighs. Close your eyes. Focus on your breath as it flows in and out. Listen to yourself inhaling and exhaling. Your conscious mind will try to fill the silence with chatter. As each thought arrives repeat 'Wel-come. Wel-go' while you continue to follow your rhythmic breathing. The gaps between your thoughts become longer. Relaxation and tapping into your inner space of stillness improves productivity, problem solving, clarity, creativity and intuition – all by doing nothing.

9. Know your values

It is in extreme moments you really find out your values. What do you love doing? When you have had a peak positive experience in the past, what values were being satisfied? What about peak negative experiences? What values were being violated? Now imagine having a business that taps into the key values of its staff and customers? What would that look like? Create a value statement for your organization – a blueprint for future recruitment. Live your company values and spread the word to cultivate the culture.

10. Choose change, not insanity

So, you have moved to a situation of seeing the problem and an understanding that you do have the power to change. The next stage is to ensure that the disempowering pattern is discontinued. Actually, you do have a choice. You decide to repeat the pattern and end up in what is popularly described as the insanity loop, where you do the same thing over and over again expecting a different result. Or you can decide and commit to change, and choose a more empowering pattern. A pattern works very like a muscle – the more you use it, the stronger it gets. The more attention you give to a thought or the more you repeat a pattern, the stronger the connections become in your nervous system. The next time you find yourself faced with a challenge, stop yourself reacting without thinking and then choose differently.

11. Seize the moment

Here are some guidelines with respect to effective complaints handling to move your customer further along the continuum between customer and friend.

If the scale of the complaint means that the employee needs to seek counsel with a superior, communication is key. The customer must be kept informed and told when they can expect a resolution of the issue. Xceptional execution of the planned resolution allows you to really start building bridges.

DO! Take the rap over seemingly 'unreasonable' complaints.

DO! Empower at source. Ritz-Carlton authorizes employees to deal with any problem at source and to implement or create any customer satisfaction solution that will cost under $2,000.

DO! Communicate, communicate, communicate.

DO! Take action.

12. Host idea sessions

Ideas are the lifeblood of any business trying to differentiate in the marketplace. At your fingertips and within your circles you have access to an abundance of ideas at minimal or zero cost.

Try a rent-a-crowd session to generate new ideas. Invite a small group from diverse backgrounds to brainstorm. The rules are simple: Every idea and opinion is noted and honored regardless of how ridiculous it may seem. This allows for free flow and potential association. The next step is to harvest and review these ideas, then report back to the idea donors what is the appropriate follow up action.

An alternative approach is to reach out online. Some argue that electronic brainstorming is best as in the normal scenario oftentimes the more vocal colleagues take the airtime and the ideas remain undiscovered.

13. Manage those moments

Get a piece of paper and highlight all the contact points between your business and the client. Be forensic. For example, how long it takes to answer the phone or follow up on a sales inquiry received via email and so on. Set standards for each of the interactions, Use existing ones or benchmark off best practice.

Then aim to exceed these on a daily basis. Consider going one stage further by guaranteeing service levels for each contact points. This could give you a competitive edge within the marketplace. Guarantees make it easier for customers to buy from you.

14. The art of sales

- Selling is still the lifeblood of most organizations. Internally we sell ideas and externally we sell products and services.
- Turn up before or on time unless you want to show disrespect to the client.
- Remember the presentation isn't about you, it's about the client. Give them an opportunity to shine. Focus laser-like on each of their words. Interject when and only when the time is right.
- If you are funny, a little humor goes a long way when you are building relationships. If you are not, please don't attempt.
- If in the first two minutes they appear disinterested, honor it and get out. It may just be that they are distracted but acknowledgements like, 'I can see you are busy at the moment, do you want me to reschedule?' will show your professionalism and get them reengaged. Speaking with someone who is not listening isn't a good strategy.
- If the client likes to talk, let them talk. When they feel good, they are more likely to buy from you. This can be a challenge

for the chatty salesperson. We are operating in an attention deficit society so giving attention is a huge rapport tool. Interject with questions, including your key selling points and allow the client to chat again.

- Keep a close eye at all times on the client's physiology. It is telling you all you need to know and will lead you flawlessly through the sale.
- Don't go with a canned presentation. Go with a personality and two ears. Craft your pitch around their unique needs.
- Use multi media. Some people like to listen, others like to see things, while others like to mess around with the product. People tend to favor one more than the other.
- There is no closing strategy. This is the logical conclusion of a good sales pitch.
- Keep it real. Only approach situations where you can add real value. Long term you won't convert customers into friends if you have just fooled them.
- Be passionate and energetic about the product or service. If you as a start-up or SME owner aren't enthusiastic, well, finish this sentence yourself.

15. Delay your vision

Scenario 1: The owner was a visionary and saw the future very clearly, even down to the finest details, including a strong business plan, the type of employees they wanted to recruit, the target audience and customer profiles.

Scenario 2: The owner brought to the company lots of enthusiasm and a desire to execute and learn by doing. They had no clue of where they were going, had no business plan and no refined idea to start or at best a loose one.

If you believe that Scenario 1 is the most realistic profile of entrepreneurs that created sustainable, disruptive businesses, you would be wrong with the occasional exception. This is contrary to the 'Hollywood version' that appears to suggest we all have a dream and a compelling vision to start. Replace the word 'visionary' with 'potterer'and you have a more realistic view.

Begin with basic sketches of the vision for the business and life you want. It may be blurred at the start. What does it look like? Imagine your lifestyle and business five months, three years and five years in the future. Who will be on your team? What type of culture will you create? Be open to a flash of genius on your path, but don't wait around for it. You don't need to know 'how' at the start, you just need to act. Don't over analyze. Too much knowledge is a dangerous thing. When you execute the magic happens. Allow your vision to adapt and grow over time. Get everyone involved. Embrace the xceptional execution ethos and see where it takes you – xceptional execution = opportunity

11
THE XCEPTIONALISTS

Asthma Care – Galway, Ireland

Balsamiq – Bologna, Italy

Blo Blow Dry Bar – Vancouver, Canada

Business Model You – Portland, USA

Dwolla – Des Moines, USA

Globant – Buenos Aires, Argentina

Outfit 7 – Limassol, Cyprus

Unislim – Newry, Northern Ireland

WeDemand – Rio de Janeiro, Brazil

ASTHMA CARE – GALWAY, IRELAND

I followed Patrick McKeown's business closely over the years. It took great courage to start, and Patrick has had many obstacles to overcome on his way. For example, taking on the might of the medical profession and pharmaceutical industry with a limited budget is an ambitious challenge. However, he has persevered to become an expert in a very technical field and in the process is making a major impact around the world. His passion for learning and sharing his skills is infectious. As a solopreneur, his story is fascinating.

Patrick explains, "Every cloud has a silver lining, and solving the very challenge which life had thrown at me led to a career infused with experience, belief and passion. From a very young age I remember wheezing and being caught for breath. Getting a good night's sleep wasn't an option as I coughed and spluttered my way through it. Even walking more than a few hundred yards was an issue.

The diagnosis was asthma and the obvious solution was medication. By the time I was in my early twenties, my condition was getting progressively worse. The amount of medication required to maintain control had increased relentlessly. I had tried everything from Acupuncture to Chinese medicine to the Alexander Technique in search of a natural solution to no avail. In 1997, I graduated from Trinity College Dublin and entered middle management for a US multinational. It was about the same time that I stumbled across an article about a Russian doctor, Konstantin Buteyko, who claimed to know how to reverse the cause of asthma. Logically it made sound sense – breathe through your nose only to filter and condition incoming air, and practice breathing exercises designed to calm breathing towards normal.

Using Buteyko's Method my asthma improved dramatically. No longer was I constantly fighting for breath, nor did I require medication. Two years on, I was living an asthma free existence."

WHEN DID YOU DECIDE TO TAKE THIS PATH?

"While my health had improved, my career had not. To be frank, I didn't like my job at all. I didn't like the systems and procedures that controlled me. My creativity was stifled and I craved for independence.

Driving home one weekend in the midst of my despair, the thought struck me that asthmatics should be made aware of correct breathing and other lifestyle factors. There was no doubt that it worked. I myself was the proof. That formed the backbone of my drive and determination. The Buteyko Method had delivered on many levels to me. I had totally eliminated the need for medication. I was sleeping better and my energy and fitness levels had been enhanced.

Add the fact that in 2002 there were 475,000 asthmatics in Ireland and this was a viable business opportunity. That weekend was a momentous one. It felt as though a weight had been lifted off me. Even though I had not thought about the intricacies of starting a business, I had an overwhelming feeling that everything was going to be all right."

WHAT CHALLENGES LAY AHEAD?

"I was going down the road less travelled, which in retrospect appeared to have unfixable craters along the way. The first major obstacle was the status quo. For anyone suffering with asthma, the conditioned response was to seek medication. Most of the research in this area was funded by medical companies. The umbrella organizations that existed to help and educate patients were funded yes, by the medical companies as well. Finally, even the education system focused on showing students pharmacological interventions to the issue of asthma.

I realized that complementary medicine often came with negative connotations. And the lack of clinical trials to back up my work meant there was a strong possibility I wouldn't be taken seriously. However, it felt right and I was living proof that this natural solution worked. I was up for the fight."

WHAT WAS YOUR INITIAL INVESTMENT?

"With working capital of $6,500 I started my business. Asthma Care was founded to enable asthmatics to learn breathing exercises to overcome their condition. I was now my own boss, free from internal office politics, from external weekly targets that increased perpetually and free from systems and controls, which stifled my creativity and initiative.

I contacted the Buteyko Clinic of Russia and by 2002 had completed my training under the tutelage of Dr. Konstantin Buteyko himself. The cost of training and travel was $4,500. With now only $2,000 left, I shared my office to mitigate costs."

DID YOU EVER THINK IT WAS NOT WORTH THE STRESS?

"I experienced many moments of doubt during my early days. Thankfully I found relief from the very therapy I was teaching. Fear, which is anguish for the future, and stress, which is anguish in the present moment, are subjective characteristics unique to each individual. Some people worry over the slightest thing, while others are calm in the face of calamity. Of course there are times in business when stress levels increase, and this can be a great driver in the short term. No job or business is worth an exchange for mental health problems, high blood pressure, chronic fatigue or even cancer."

HOW DID YOU PROMOTE THE BUSINESS ON A LIMITED BUDGET?

"I set about getting as much free publicity as possible as advertising rates were prohibitive. After two months I got my first big PR break being featured on the local paper. This got me my first three clients and so the journey began. Most of the journalists wanted proof that it worked, so patients were rolled out. We met and beat the challenge every time. My first book Asthma Free Naturally was self-published in 2003. Such was its success, I was offered a worldwide deal from Harper Collins in 2005. Over the next few years, I published six other titles, including bestsellers Close Your Mouth and Anxiety Free: Stop Worrying and Quiet Your Mind, in addition to producing a bestselling range of DVDs. Within that time period I travelled the world training practitioners in this field."

HOW DID YOUR OTHER IDEAS EVOLVE?

"An interesting pattern emerged over the past few years. Though I enjoyed and reviewed all the research being conducted around the world on a daily basis through my Google alerts, more and more of my ideas began to surface from working with patients. In the questionnaires they completed, many reported substantial improvement in other conditions following attendance at the clinics including snoring, insomnia and obstructive sleep apnea. These ideas were to add further options to my services. Honoring this, in 2007, I founded Snoring.ie to deliver non-invasive, breathing techniques to unblock the nose and restore breathing to calm normal levels. Between my clients and networking with top practitioners from around the world in related fields, my courses evolved to cater for a variety of ailments: asthma, sleep problems, anxiety, stress, prevention of crooked teeth and improved sports performance."

WHAT'S YOUR VALUE PROPOSITION?

"I was acutely aware of the prohibitive medical costs of the ailment. Approximately $1,500 is spent annually on medication and this doesn't take into account days lost at school or at work and the reduced quality of life costs. That's why I was adamant that Asthma Care would offer a more cost effective alternative. From a $10 book to a $250 course, we aim to cater for all income classes. Indeed it is my policy never to refuse anyone on economic grounds. I understand where they're at, and more importantly, I know where they can go on this journey. That is my focus: Delivering life-changing exercises at a value for money price."

WHAT'S YOUR TAKE ON XCEPTIONAL EXECUTION?

"Utilizing all avenues available to better meet the expectations and demands of customers. This comes easy when one is passionate about their work. I love my job. It is not an effort to get up of a Monday morning. Nor is it an effort to stay focused, driven and motivated. My primary motivators are independence, happiness and to provide value to others."

ASTHMA CARE TAKEAWAYS

- Pain could be the catalyst for that business idea.
- Committing to action lifts a huge weight off your shoulders.
- If it feels right, it is right.
- Don't focus on the obstacles before you take that first step.
- Calming the mind is the key to sanity and clarity.
- You don't need a big budget to make a big impact.
- Execution creates opportunities – all you need to do is ask.
- What's the worst possible scenario or the best, in the context of you growing or starting the business?

BALSAMIQ – BOLOGNA, ITALY

It is not often a site on its own inspires you to want to know more about an organization but such was the case with Balsamiq. Gary, my Australian based book project manager suggested a visit and I was immediately drawn to the friendly, inviting face of the company. It certainly wasn't what I expected but I soon discovered that there is a method in their warm approach. From zero sales to 150,000 units in 4 years was quite an accomplishment for the self-professed lifestyle business. Where many companies struggled for finance, Balsamiq had a line of VCs waiting outside their door. They decided instead to grow organically.

When I heard Balsamiq's CEO Peldi keynote at a conference, I loved his honesty, energy and simplicity. Much could be learned from his journey. Giacomo 'Peldi' Guilizzoni admits, "I came from your standard Italian middle class family. My mother and father split up when I was two, and then both remarried so I had a very extended family. As an aside a lot of successful entrepreneurs come from broken marriages. They say they have something to prove and this is their motivation. I don't know if that is the case with me.

My dad had his own insurance agency. In an attempt to automate as much as he could, he bought this big old computer in 1986. The computer came with one programmer. There were no software packages at that time. In school I had a love of maths and computers, so I was delighted to receive from my dad my very own copy of *How to Learn Basic*, a computer language book, at the age of twelve. Soon I was able to program onto that big floppy disk and, to my complete pleasure, appeared to be able to tell the machine what I wanted it to do. This was a major moment in my life. I valued the opportunity to be able to be in control of something.

My dad had an intense hatred of working for other people. One key thing I learned from him was the need to work hard to achieve. My mother was always very warm and generous – a real people's person. She was also very carefree. I have no doubt my mother's generosity showed me the way in terms of donating software to as many people as possible."

HOME FROM HOME?

"At the age of 17, after finishing high school, I visited San Francisco and felt totally at home. San Francisco was the place – all the major computer giants had some presence there. This allowed me the opportunity to learn from the best in the business. Reluctantly I returned to the University of Bologna to finish my studies. – I did my thesis on a piece of software called 'Director', which had been developed by Macromedia. When I returned to California the following year, my goal was to work for them. I went directly to their HR department and looked for an opportunity. As it turned out the perfect job that focused around my thesis work was available. Macromedia of course were subsequently taken over by Adobe."

WHAT INSPIRED BALSAMIQ?

"The idea I had was for mockups – an idea I had for some time at Adobe. Very simply, mockups solved an existing problem I had. In meetings I liked to sketch things out because I just think that way. At the bottom of the sketch you would always write, 'Do not erase' on the board until you got back to take a picture or copy it down. The proposed product would help to solve this. It would be a graphical tool that allowed people to sketch user interface for whatever the person wanted, be it a website or a piece of software which could then be shared in real time. I decided to do 20 minutes of research and found little competition. This was the motivation for me following the path.

  I now know that if I dug a little deeper at that time, I would have found better potential competitors and have been dissuaded. Good competitors, but they still hadn't our angle. In retrospect, my naïveté was useful because it would have be daunting to know then what I know now in terms of the type of effort required. I accept of course the '10 percent inspiration 90 percent perspiration' theory and that luck may be where hard work meets opportunity. However, one could argue there was some luck in how I started."

DOES FEAR COME INTO PLAY?

"Probably the greatest fear I have is that we lose the family feel to our business, in the way we work together and the relationships we have with our customers. We work hard to keep this going with a huge focus on customer service plus only recruiting people to what they describe as their dream job. So now we are a big restaurant on the web with 150,000 customers and sixteen employees. In some respects I work hard to ensure we grow as slowly and as solidly as we can. This flies in the face of what is described as your hot start-up by Paul Graham, who suggests that you should grow 10 fold in five years. So in essence, we are not a start-up."

DO YOU WORRY ABOUT COMPETITION?

"One thing you should not fear is competition. They only help to raise your game and build a better product. If they are better than you, you deserve to lose. We had a funny story about our first ever sale. We were due to launch but got our first sale from the website three days early. Even though the website was up and the payment system live, we hadn't informed the bloggers or told the community that we were live. I remember putting the receipt on the wall to honor the achievement. A few months later we got a contact from a customer suggesting we should add a project management feature and a web app. As my plan all along was to be a one-man show, I knew and explained that his wasn't possible. A few months later we stumbled on this company that had cloned our software and had added a project management feature and a website app. They were indeed our first customer and became our competitor. It was time to take down the receipt. Their business is no more."

THEY SAY WHEN YOU GIVE OUT, YOU GET BACK. THIS APPEARS TO BE A BIG PART OF YOUR STRATEGY?

"We give away our software to around 40 organizations each day. The software mainly goes to non-profit organizations but also to anyone who shows they are doing a good deed. One that comes to mind was a request from a man who was designing a site for an orphanage in Ecuador. We were delighted to help. At the start we gave the software away to bloggers and all we demanded in return was an honest review. We were happy to do all this because it wasn't about the money. We did know that with all the feedback we could develop something that would make us a living in the end."

AS LEARNING IS YOUR KEY GOAL, HOW DO YOU FIND TIME TO CONTINUALLY SHARPEN THE SAW?

"In the last five years, I have been constantly over my head in terms of the business, constantly having to roll up my sleeves to work on a different challenge, one coming after the next. Though I may not have the time to read as many books as I like, I am fully immersed in ongoing learning 24/7. I don't suspect that this will continue in the long term at this intensity but for now all my brainpower is invested. I am definitely learning loads from the University of the Customer, the Coworker and the Community."

ARE YOU ABLE TO SWITCH OFF?

"It is hard to switch off but I am trying. Normally I watch a Canadian program on how things are made. It is really boring and puts me to sleep or some Formula One Racing that I have recorded. In our next retreat, I am inviting someone to teach us the art of meditation. I am very fascinated about this topic. I am always trying to be more present, to be more in the moment when I am with my child. Meditation should help in this respect."

NEW PROJECTS IN THE PIPELINE?

"I try very hard not to be distracted by new ideas as our time is firmly focused on developing our existing product. However, I have a read-only file full of product ideas. When Mockups is well developed we will look at these. This could happen next year, but don't hold your breath. I said that four years ago. As part of our mission to rid the world of bad software, it is obviously part of our remit to look at better and new ways of doing things."

BEST APPS FOR ENTREPRENEURS?

"Some of the tools I have found invaluable as we built the business are Google Apps, Dropbox, Atlassian Confluence – our internal wiki, Hipchat, Pivotaltracker and Desk.com."

WHAT LESSONS WOULD YOU TEACH YOUR CHILD?

"My son GJ goes to the International School in Bologna. During induction, I listened to the principal telling parents that most of us have probably ended up in a job that didn't exist when we were born. He added that this was likely to be the case when our children reached their working career so what their focus would be is on developing the child, developing his ability to work as part of a team and how to speak in public. This really struck a chord with me. I have very little to add to this except that I would like to help him find his passion because we live at a time when he can monetize it. I of course want to teach him to be a good person, a good citizen, respectful, hardworking and principled. Part of me would love it if he took over from me, but if he wants to be a rock star, that's fine by me."

YOUR TAKE ON XCEPTIONAL EXECUTION?

"Build something that (a) it gets talked about a lot and (b) our competitors want to copy because that means we are the thought leaders. It is so good it gets copied. It is about infusing character into all of your outputs. So as a simple example, we want to have a face on every page of our website and all our social pages."

BALSAMIQ TAKEAWAYS

- No overnight success. Peldi has been programming since the age of 12.
- Go for gold. He wanted to work for Macromedia and went for it on stepping on US soil.
- When he set his start-up goal, circumstances conspired to make it happen – 'a cosmic thing' as he said himself.
- The business idea was a solution to an existing problem.
- His major goal was to learn – he had legislated for failure.
- Fear can be healthy and should be respected.
- Recruit people to their dream job.
- Customer service can be your competitive edge in the software market.
- Failure is good as long as you take responsibility and fix the problem.
- Xceptional execution is about infusing character into all of your outputs.

BLO BLOW DRY BAR – VANCOUVER, CANADA

In an attempt to get the best interviewees around the world, I reached out to my tribe and asked people to recommend potential Xceptionalists. Ms. Mary Marcus, business consultant, told me about Devon Brooks who transformed an ordinary idea, blow-drying hair, into a business empire through xceptional execution. She remarkably achieved during an incredibly difficult time in her life, as a few years previously she was the victim of two violent assaults. I marveled at her resilience, commitment and drive.

Devon says, "When I was in my second year in college at the London College of Fashion, I was talking on the phone to my mother who was attending one of the big 'women in business' events in Canada. We had a laugh about how terrible and exhausted some of the women looked. And in the department of vanity, the problem for these and so many others was that there wasn't enough time in the day to indulge in a 1 hour 45 min task of a wash and blow dry.

The costs were prohibitive. At an average of $65 plus VAT a pop, then multiply that by three times a week, and you are spending a lot of money and time. The only other option was enduring the torture of holding a blow dryer to your hair for 45 minutes without breaking a sweat before your big meeting. Meanwhile research at that time asserted that having great hair was what made women feel the most confident and self-assured.

There was nothing in the market servicing this niche. This was the background for my second year university project; from there I conceptualized an answer to solve a hairy problem for busy women."

DID YOU FORESEE THE POTENTIAL?

"When I wrote the business plan, I envisioned the brand becoming the 'Starbucks of the beauty regime'. That vision wasn't just about scale, it was about the congruency of the experience. We shared that vision with our team, at every level.

Within six months we were opening our first Blo Blow Dry Bar in Yaletown, Vancouver, in the midst of the recession. Our launch party was a smash with 500 media and special guests. Franchise requests poured in. Within the year we had received hundreds of franchise requests to expand Blo internationally. We'd hit a chord even before people had truly experienced our service. Everyone said to us, 'I swear I thought of that first'. It was truly an ordinary idea, we just executed it.

One of our first cadets, the name we gave our clients, was a very well known broadcaster from Vancouver. She told us a story that reflected our confidence in this new direction. She explained that in her line of work she could literally be sharing the most important breaking news story of her career and the majority of the comments that the network would receive would be about her hairstyle.

People say 'don't judge a book by its cover', but in a world of overexposure, sometimes your 'cover' – the periphery – is your first and only chance to get the attention you deserve. That applies to the individual in the same way as it does to a company. At some point what you want needs to become what others see as well. We are after all a very visual society."

DID THE TRADITIONAL HAIR SALON
WELCOME YOU TO THE MARKET?

"Despite our best efforts to educate the 'styling community' about who we were and how we'd be of value to them, we had many neighboring salon owners who didn't get it. They would use our core brand color, magenta, and advertise "Cheap blow-drys here." The funny thing was we weren't really competition because salons used blow-drying as more of a training opportunity for juniors than a revenue stream.

We ignited a market category. I've loved seeing new companies interpret this concept and enter the marketplace. Since 2007 as the Blo Blow Dry Bar brand has grown globally, we have also watched other blow dry bars pop up around the world – some of them a little more original than others."

THE POSITIVE SIDE OF COMPETITION?

"Competition gives us choices. And consumers want their say. That's why companies like Kickstarter have taken off and soared.

There is room in the blow dry bar category for all.

A week after I submitted my business plan, Sir Philip Green was opening a blow dry bar in Top Shop. I thought it was extremely cool that we were on the same wavelength as him. Ideas are just ideas, what matters is execution."

YOUR BRANDING IS SUPERB – COULD YOU BREAK IT DOWN?

"Our focus was on turning the session styling model on its head. At the end of the experience we wanted cadets looking like they had just come off a catwalk and feeling a million dollars. Fast and affordable catwalk quality was our standard. With this in mind we started to build the brand. We had franchise and brand manuals before we even opened our front doors. We were in this to grow.

We created Blo U, Blo's 'University' to train up the stylists on our hair menu's key offerings. We had created our own Blocabulary. The floor manager was the Blo Boss. The session stylists were Bloers. The franchisees loved the process of coining themselves with their own blo-name like, the Head Mistress or the Queen Coiffeur. All of this was a part of the backbone of the brand.

In terms of decision-making, we channeled the Blo Girl – she was our target audience. Whatever decision we made, be it about a store layout or a piece of furniture, we pondered on what the Blo Girl would prefer. One aspect of our brand that earned us some solid buzz was our domain name. We bought 'www.blomedry.com'. We wanted the domain name to be action-based – like, this is what we do. There was some hysterical media hype, and journalists would email us the funniest stories of what happened when they went to the other 'blow' websites which were all slightly raunchy. We knew that would happen. It was just another element of the playfulness of the brand."

YOU'VE CONFRONTED FEAR IN YOUR LIFE?

"I make a personal commitment to myself on this. I will never let fear stop me from taking action. The most fearless people I know aren't untouchable. They are those who look fear right in the eye and do what they are committed to in spite of it."

HOW DID YOUR PARENTS INFLUENCE YOU?

"My parents divorced when I was seven years of age. My mum, Judy Brooks, has had a profound influence on my life. She was a hustler and an entrepreneur by necessity. She had to make ends meet to put food on the table. We didn't come from wealth, and she never had the luxury of getting much help when I was young. She ran a company, taught as a fitness instructor and did whatever she needed to do to earn a living. All I had to do to figure out what drive was, was to look at my mum. Gratefully, I didn't have to become an entrepreneur to survive. But we are two peas in a pod, and I like to think I got some of her best qualities, including her smile and laughter.

"My dad on the other hand was very difficult, yet in a strange way was a great teacher. We haven't had a relationship since I was about 15. It was heartbreaking for me for years. But after many incidents and interactions where he showcased his lack of integrity or care something finally dawned on me. 'If he wasn't my dad I wouldn't put up with this,' I thought. I felt what many people feel who have challenges with family. 'He's my dad so I HAVE to work this out, I have to try.'

I knew deep down that the right thing to do was to walk away. I didn't like how I felt when he was around and I certainly didn't like what it brought out in me. I didn't know it then, but I was making a values based decision. I wasn't choosing not to have a relationship with my dad. I was choosing integrity, congruency and joy."

ARE VALUES A DEAL BREAKER OR MAKER FOR YOU?

"Values are my filter. They are deal makers or breakers. The expectation isn't that we never slip up or make mistakes. The expectation is that when we do screw up, we acknowledge it, take responsibility and then move on graciously. I get really annoyed when someone behaves completely different to how they portray themselves.

I have never experienced regret over a values-based decision.

Blo was a fantastic learning experience. It was like an MBA, an incredible high, and a vessel that allowed me to support causes I passionately believe in. Overall it gave me a huge platform for the rest of my career, and a few extraordinary friendships."

ADVICE FOR ENTREPRENEURS?

"It is always natural for me to look for answers, so entrepreneurship will always be a part of my adventure in life. Entrepreneurship is a way to solve problems. It is a vessel for ground level change."

BLO BLOW DRY BAR TAKEAWAYS

- Even a solution to an age-old problem can convert into a business empire. You can blow customers away.
- Articulate a vision, and communicate it to your team.
- Your brand is your vibe. It's how you make people feel.
- Fearlessness is not being without fear, but acting in spite of it.
- Your values are your filters, deal makers and breakers. Don't apologize for standing by your values.
- Work and life are not separate. Write your 'time-out' into your master plan.
- Intuition is useless without listening and responsiveness.

BUSINESS MODEL YOU – PORTLAND, OREGON, USA

Tim Clark is a teacher, trainer, author, entrepreneur and former university professor. He has authored or edited five books on entrepreneurship, business models, and personal development, including the international bestsellers Business Model You and Business Model Generation, which together have sold half a million copies in 26 countries. In the prevailing attention deficit market Tim's one page personal business model approach resonates. Add in the fact that he sold his own business in a multi-million dollar deal, I was very clear that his ideas would add real value to *DO! the pursuit of xceptional execution*.

Tim Clark shares, "I was the son of two teachers. My father was a dual professor, Aeronautics and Astronautics and Electrical Engineering, and my mother was an elementary school teacher. It does appear I was destined to be a teacher.

I was an introvert and painfully shy as a teenager and young man. I tried to compensate for this through various types of performance. Before, during and after university I was involved in performance-related ventures, including vaudeville and rock 'n roll music. The live entertainment industry is a creative, unstructured environment. Once I tasted that kind of freedom and excitement, it was hard to get enthusiastic about traditional work. After working as a musician it got hard to become enthusiastic about being broke all the time and working at night.

In college I studied psychology, and one of the modules I chose to complete my graduation credits was Japanese. I had a fantastic teacher and gravitated toward Japanese language studies, subsequently moving there. As soon as I had enough skills as a translator, I went freelance. Translating built my writing, editing, and localization skills.

Along the way I became a very heavy PC and email user. After many temp jobs I ended up working for Eastman Kodak in a job I can only describe as completely out of sync with who I was."

WHY ENTREPRENEURSHIP?

"I became an entrepreneur for the most common reason that people become entrepreneurs: I prefer working for myself. I'm a firm believer that entrepreneurship is based on hard skills, experience and creating market value, not 'ideas' per se.

In 1994, I launched the Do-it-Yourself Import Center, an online Japanese language resource for consumers who wanted to bypass middlemen to purchase directly from overseas sources. That was the natural consequence of having strong Japanese language reading, writing and translation skills plus plenty of experience with computers and email and putting it all together to create something that people valued. The idea was modestly important, however, the skills and experience behind it were crucial. It all started from there.

I don't believe I had anything in particular that enabled me to make it as an entrepreneur. About the only thing I can say is common to all entrepreneurs is that they are willing to work hard. I like to say, 'If you want to work like a human being, get a job. If you want to work like a farm animal, become an entrepreneur.'

My main motivation was intense curiosity about the Internet, and specifically about why there was almost no Japanese language world wide web content to be seen in the fall of 1994. I instantly decided to devote most of my waking hours to figuring out why there was no such content, and how I could create it. That was my 'aha' moment. I wasn't thinking about making money. If I'd been thinking about making money, I wouldn't have done it. I was just extremely curious, and completely excited by it. It was the most amazing thing I'd ever seen."

DID YOU EXPERIENCE FEAR?

"The fear of having a boring life is why I have always wanted to do fun and exciting things. That's why I found working at Kodak, a wonderful company, hidebound to an unsustainable business model, boring and it was not for me."

WHAT'S YOUR TAKE ON XCEPTIONAL EXECUTION?

"It means doing things for the right reasons more than doing things right. You can screw up and then fix your execution but you can't really change your fundamental reasons for doing something. For example – and most of your readers won't recall this – in the early days of commercial dial-up internet access, there was a tool called Majordomo. Basically it was a way to send out bulk email messages to a subscriber list. But if you failed to send the initial message correctly, it could create an evil email loop whereby everyone on the list got the same message over and over, including all the subsequent complaints and unsubscribe requests – including their own – in an endless, upward spiraling email bomb.

One day, as the proprietor of a several thousand person opt-in list, I made the fatal mistake and found myself the subject of ferocious complaints and angry subscribers. I immediately called my ISP and had them shut it off. They were plenty upset too. I apologized sheepishly to my subscribers. The point is that my intentions were good and I wasn't trying to spam people. It was an honest mistake, and our subscribers forgave us. Our execution was lousy, but our fundamental reasons were good. We were trying to help people. Indeed my definition of work is just that – trying to help other people.

In Business Model You we talk a lot about purpose. Truly, I see it as a very misunderstood concept. When people hear 'purpose' they immediately think of the need to help homeless or sick children or something selfless and altruistic. Purpose can be much more ordinary, much more local. If we link our purpose to our work we are assured of authenticity. Too often people don't link purpose to work, looking at the big scheme as opposed to the small actions they can take to help."

LUCK, OR DOES FORTUNE FAVOR THE PREPARED?

"I'm not an operations guy, so I'm not one to advise on xceptional execution. I've always simply blundered ahead and muddled through. I've been lucky in recognizing opportunity, even when I didn't know how to exploit it. I just walked in the direction of interesting areas and made something happen. Ultimately I guess you make your own luck, but I certainly feel I was very lucky. In 1997 Amazon asked us to design their first Japanese site. One person may say we were lucky, or you could see it as the result of competence and xceptional execution."

IS VISION OVERRATED?

"Having a vision is easy, anyone can do it. Designing specific ways to achieve something on the other hand is difficult. What excites the media is that someone has a great idea and makes millions as a result. The reality is, that it rarely happens. It is competency that unlocks a person's potential. Designing processes, structures or strategies to achieve challenging goals is difficult. Few people can do that well. My 'vision' so to speak is the same as my value proposition: Help others advance in their careers."

HOW IMPORTANT IS SELF-AWARENESS?

"Action produces more self-awareness and insight than introspection. A certain level of success produces situations that demand greater self-awareness. If you grow a business to the point where it needs professional management, you will quickly discover whether or not you have the ability and/or appetite to be a manager and I discovered that I lacked both. Knowing early on what you're good at – and not so good at – is a huge help. That requires self-awareness."

DO YOU TAKE TIME FOR TIMEOUT?

"I always forget about upcoming vacations and my wife has to remind me. I'm lousy at scheduling time out but I'm very good at taking time out of every day to think or read."

BUSINESS MODEL YOU TAKEAWAYS

- A good teacher in school or college may have a bigger impact than you think.
- Entrepreneurship is based on hard skills, not ideas.
- If you want to work like a farm animal, be an entrepreneur.
- Feel the fear and don't do it anyway unless you have the competency.
- Don't spend your life being bored.
- Vision is overrated.

- Purpose is more ordinary than you think.
- Celebrate – someone has just paid attention.
- Go with your gut.
- Doing more than reflecting is better for developing self awareness.
- Thinking is for cowards.

DWOLLA – DES MOINES, USA

A colleague on the Net Minds team nominated Dwolla as an Xceptionalist. Due diligence presented an opportunity to understand the thinking of someone whose goal is to create a global clearing house offering consumers and businesses a brilliant payment system that could end our dependence on credit cards. CEO Ben Milne strikes me as brilliant, understated, clear and focused.

Ben shares, "My dad was a dentist and my mother a stay at home mum. I have one sister. My father was a great role model. From a very early age he wanted me to earn my own money. This was the start of my entrepreneurial life. I did what so many people did around my age and started a lawn boy business. This experience taught me all the necessary aspects of the business – going to customers who could afford the service, promoting the business, giving them the necessary documentation, receipts and so on. For $25 I would mow your lawn, oftentimes throwing in a trim in the bargain.

My family had provided me with my first car so I could use the money to fund my discretionary purchases like stereos, computers, software etc. When I was a teenager my dad got Parkinson's disease, which caused him to retire early from his dental practice. That didn't stop him from his entrepreneurial pursuits. He invested in a big real estate development which gave the town its first soccer pitch. The latter happened just as I had finished graduate school. So it was very timely and I was really proud. You couldn't but be inspired by him. Even today he is a medical miracle. He has just gone through brain surgery and added five quality years to his life."

WHAT WAS YOUR FIRST SIGNIFICANT ENTREPRENEURIAL ADVENTURE?

"In 1999 I designed a website for a few thousand dollars for a shop. In lieu of payment they gave me credits on products. I then proceeded to create an e-commerce car audio site. I started Elemental Designs, offering only six speakers in the range and built it to a $1.5 million business. I loved the independence of it.

I knew dropping out of college was the right idea because if I had stayed, it would only have ended up wasting my parents a lot of money. I hadn't the heart for it and really struggled. I was much more motivated by working with customers and earning a living. Of course my family wasn't happy with my decision but in time they came around. It was hard for them to accept their child turning his back on the route that made them successful, one their parents never had the opportunity to pursue."

WHAT WAS THE INSPIRATION BEHIND DWOLLA?

"I looked everywhere and tried everything to see how the exorbitant credit card costs in my speaker business could be mitigated. I read the early days of PayPal and ACH. Then I came up with the idea and pitched the bank.

We created a working software platform and spent the next year and a half learning how to do this legally. We launched in December 2010. Since then we have made significant progress and are now bigger than many regional banks. We have gone from 'We really hope this works' to 'This thing has legs' to 'We wonder how far we can take it' to 'Now we are looking how we can speed up things'. We are confident as we are so far ahead with our technology and distribution of it. We acknowledge its uniqueness and we know the outcome is inevitable."

HERE TODAY, GONE TODAY – LIVE LIFE NOW … IS THAT YOUR STRATEGY?

"Life is short. My mother got cancer and survived it, my dad Parkinson's, and my mum's friend died from cancer – there are a million unknowns. So it is clear there is no better time than now. You can decide today what you want to do now. You may not have this privilege tomorrow. Entrepreneurship is definitely something everybody should try out at some point in their life."

WHAT MOTIVATES YOU?

"The younger I was, the more I was motivated by money. Now I love the opportunity to make an impact. You know it is the same amount of work on a potentially $1 billion business or a few hundred thousand dollars turnover, so why not put yourself into the one where you can make the most difference, make people's lives better, put some dollars back in their pockets. We are definitely going to create more value than we take out.

Look at the figures – $40 billion annually on interchange fees in the US alone. Imagine that back in people's pockets. That would make a difference. Imagine in developing economies to put those fees back in their pockets – it could mean a bigger house.

Dwolla is part of a logical evolution, just like email is replacing physical mail and VOIP and mobile replacing landlines. And in our model everyone wins except the stakeholders in the old system. Home is wherever you are – I don't have an office in Iowa or New York. I just come with a backpack and computer."

TOO MUCH KNOWLEDGE IS A BAD THING – DO YOU AGREE?

"If you have enough information, you will definitely see the difficulties. You will be more inclined to stay with and justify the status quo. Remember part of doing something new is changing the information that fed into the past decision. Not understanding anything about banking was probably an advantage at the outset and indeed everyday in the office. It probably scares a lot of people but it is a platform for growth.

Information is important to manage risk. It may be okay to decide to jump off a one-story building, but not a four story one. If you are seen as someone who totally abandons any risk, you may send the wrong message to your team that you don't care for them, and you don't care for yourself, therefore you are a dangerous person to do business with."

HOW DO YOU ENHANCE THE CUSTOMER EXPERIENCE?

"Originally the idea was to create a tool that would allow for the transfer of money without any interchange fees. Then we decided to focus on the user experience, so we hired a designer because the graphics were ugly. Now our focus is on allowing people to buy whatever they want as quickly as possible. Payment should be an afterthought. At the same time we want the merchant to receive the money as quickly as possible. We are still exploring how we can achieve this outcome better and faster."

WHAT'S YOUR VISION FOR DWOLLA?

"At the outset, like any entrepreneur, you are the only one who cares about something, you do have an idea on how this could work out. But you can't do it on your own so you share it with your team so it is not misunderstood and it evolves. As the team grows, the vision evolves.

The overall vision is to be the global clearing house. As you can imagine, there are a lot of steps along the way. First up is to get a share of the market in the US. Then identify the correct international market strategy – is it Africa or Europe and so on. Now we have a plan that breaks down the following two to three years by quarters and deliverables within each in terms of all the aspects of the business. This helps in challenging us to reverse engineer to meet our targets. It also helps to make better decisions. Our investors are an excellent help at this stage as they have already walked the path of creating international businesses."

DWOLLA TAKEAWAYS

- Live life in the now.
- Take responsibility for your failures, remember you have another shot.
- Work on a project that has maximum impact.
- The biggest deals are based around relationships.
- Have people around you that you can disagree with respectfully.
- With enough information you will be more inclined to stay with and justify the status quo.
- Business isn't rocket science.
- Don't spend more money than you earn.
- You can't get what you want until your customers get what they want.
- Apologize when necessary.

GLOBANT – BUENOS AIRES, ARGENTINA

In 2012, I keynoted at a leadership conference in Argentina. Afterward I asked Julio, the conference organizer which company he thought most lived the xceptional execution ethos. Immediately he said, "Globant". Soon after, I posed the same question to another colleague Maria in Buenos Aires and she also replied, "Globant." Why? Globant shows a freshness and willingness to innovate, a desire to be and do differently. Theirs is a story that needs telling.

Guibert Englebienne, co-founder and Chief Technology Officer explains in more detail, "It was the middle of the crisis in 2002, when the peso was devalued. We decided we needed an alternative source of income. One of my partners, Martin Migoya, invested in some Indian shares that skyrocketed. At that time many companies were investing in specialized IT companies in emerging markets. These companies in turn were catalysts for the creation of a new middle class in their country.

This was our inspiration. We wanted to create a global player from Latin America, one that would make credible technology from the region that could import opportunities and export software. After a series of meetings between the four now co-founders we all quit our jobs and started the journey.

For the first time after creating six companies, I was part of a solid founding team where we are all different but complement each other. We had most of the strengths we needed: analysis, creativity and a focus on xceptional execution. First there were a lot of temptations. Most Argentinians focus on Brazil or Hispanic countries as their markets.

With the US and the UK accounting for 75 percent of the market, we decided to focus there. Headquartered in Buenos Aires, we believed companies needed an alternative to India, Israel and Ireland and that Latin America could be it. We also wanted to give our people something to be proud of. There is something weird about a country that outsources their happiness to a football team every four years. Being software engineers, what could be better than competing out there with our work?"

THE GURUS TELL US THAT FAILING TO PLAN IS PLANNING TO FAIL – DID YOU START WITH A STRONG BUSINESS PLAN?

"We did not have a business plan. With the help of Endeavor 18 months later we did a 5-year plan, which was successfully executed. We agreed where we wanted to put the bar and worked hard to achieve it. As a service organization, our attitude was to listen to our customers' needs and adapt."

HOW IMPORTANT WERE YOUR INITIAL CUSTOMERS IN GLOBANT'S BUSINESS DEVELOPMENT?

"Our customers were our best advertisements and thankfully when they moved from one job to another, they kept referring us and we got another opportunity. One of these customers moved to Google. This was to be a huge milestone in Globant's history.

After a year of an exhaustive selection process, we were chosen as the first company in Google's history for outsourcing software development. This was a significant victory for us. Suddenly, many other innovative companies wanted to also work with us. Our customers now include LinkedIn, Yahoo, Zynga, Dreamworks, Sony, Southwest Airlines, EA, Salesforce, Cisco and Autodesk among others.

The original focus was on what this industry had been doing traditionally: Increasing performance and cost reduction through technology. However, our customers were taking us to unexpected places. Rather than creating technology for running corporations, they were turning to us to create consumer facing software products. While it may seem similar, the nature is very different: Focus on design, the need to innovate and rapidly adapt to competition are some of the differentiators when creating this type of software. Now Globant specializes in creating appealing software products to reach millions of consumers. In doing so, it enables companies to establish a dialogue and to engage."

RECRUITMENT IS A KEY PART OF YOUR STRATEGY – TELL US A LITTLE ABOUT YOUR EARLY RECRUITS?

"Recently we celebrated ten years in business and Juan Umaran, our first employee, was describing how he got recruited. After a chat with Juan, our Co-Founder Martin started to play the piano.

Out of the blue, Martin asked him what was the song he was playing. Juan guessed 'Massive Attack' correctly. 'You are hired,' said Martin, and so the adventure began.

"Some time later I was interviewing another potential recruit. I spotted and highlighted a major information deficit. The interviewee confided in me that he had to take two years out to care for his sick father. I felt "this is the kind of guy I want to work with" and decided to give him another chance. By the time the next interview came Guido knew not only the technology but got connected with the ones who created it. He was recruited and became a great employee who sweated the company values."

HOW HIGH IS THE BAR?

"Today, at any given moment, we're working on approximately 400 projects across a variety of technologies. Nowadays, every company faces the challenge of engaging with consumers through technology, but those consumers are swimming in a sea of abundance.

Innovation has been democratized and as a result of this, it is now simpler, faster and cheaper to create new products, making it difficult to stay competitive. Therefore there's a pressure to innovate. We realized that what we had was a first mover advantage on every hot technology out there. The fact that we are working with the biggest companies and on so many projects allows us to stay ahead.

Our focus is now on being an innovator not just a company that meets customer demands. To facilitate this process our aim is to put innovation center stage in our culture. Through our Labs, we explore technologies our customers are not yet demanding, and through crowdsourcing from a large group of Globers, we achieve scale. The rest of the organization rapidly adopted the push for innovation. Our sales force got it.

Our communications team launched a series of innovation events which we call 'Flip Thinking'. These events focus on thinking outside the box. Speakers can come from our employees or some guests like a Chief Technology Officer from the USA, a NASA engineer or a neuroscientist."

WHAT SORT OF LESSONS COULD YOU GIVE POTENTIAL ENTREPRENEURS?

"Entrepreneurship is about freedom. Financial freedom in particular, but it is also about what you leave behind. As a leader you have a responsibility to look after others, to be a role model. We can be very proud of what we have achieved with the company, but also the success that many of the former employees have had since leaving us.

The true impact of Globant will not be Globant per-se, but the dozens of companies started by people who, working with us, learned how through hard work and ultra-competitiveness you can create long-standing organizations. It requires hard work, but it doesn't require magic.

We like to talk about importing opportunities and exporting software. An example of this was creating an office in Antarctica which was to go on to developing software. We wanted to show there are opportunities everywhere to make a difference. In that context my advice to potential entrepreneurs would be:

- Try to solve a big problem, avoid niches.
- Be extremely passionate, this is the journey of your life.
- Create a founding team that can help you make it happen. It is very hard to create a story on your own.
- Focus, focus, focus."

THE IMPORTANCE OF CULTURE SCREAMS OUT FROM YOUR WEBSITE – HOW DO YOU CREATE A COMPELLING CULTURE?

"Culture is everything and values play a major part in shaping the company culture. A leader must be a guardian of the values. Our aim is to create an environment where we can tap into the intrinsic motivation of the employees. Our management lives and breathes those values. This is not because we hire them well, but because they grow up within a company that perceives and recognizes certain behaviors.

The following have evolved after five years in business:

1. Autonomy

If you choose as much as you can about your work, you'll do it happier and with better results.

2. Mastery

Generation Y, the core of our workforce, has been born into a world where things move rapidly, so the sense of urgency to develop a good career puts an emphasis on creating an environment where you can learn and get fast feedback on what you do well.

3. Purpose

Our people know they can make an impact, not only during their free time but also as they work. So we allow for intrapreneurs who can create a real impact. As leaders we have a big dream that goes beyond an economic success. We want to be the best company in the world doing what we do.

4. Aim for excellence

Think big. Have fun. Act ethically. Be a team player. Constantly innovate. These values are printed on the wall in every office.

We have a peer to peer program called 'Stellar' which gives employees five stars that they can give out to people they see as excelling in any of the values. This system works brilliantly. Generation Y's want to see they are making a difference and having an impact. To that end they all have their social platforms. As an aside, I am sick of reading stories highlighting that employees are all about benefits, that their demands are hedonistic. Most people are more concerned about making a difference.

Through the 'Stellar' program we get an insight into who is who within the company and then elicit their opinions on how we could make Globant a better company. We never mix 'Stellar' with any monetary reward in order to keep it honest and truthful.

Technical people don't necessarily want to be in management positions. Whether they choose to be a manager or not, it is important to share their knowledge. This is why we set up an elite group within the organization, the 'Premier League'. It is a by-invitation-only group that accounts for the top 1 percent of the company's technical people. Members are peers and selected by unanimous consent.

I was the first one in the club, followed by my first choice Osvaldo. We came together and then decided who was worthy of becoming number three. Then the three of us came together to select number four and so on. The group is a great sounding board for any of the challenges we have."

WHAT IS YOUR TAKE ON XCEPTIONAL EXECUTION?

"Xceptional execution is setting a goal, getting the right team together and working very hard to achieve it. Execution brings confidence."

WHAT'S THE ROLE OF TECHNOLOGY IN YOUR COMMUNICATION STRATEGY?

"In addition to my role as Chief Technology Officer, I am a sociologist and keenly interested in the science of motivation and how people connect to each other. We are continually looking at how we communicate as a community, both individually and collectively. In the process we obviously review how technology enhances or disrupts the communication process.

We recently launched a new app – Next2You. Originally the idea was for carpooling so Globers knew who lived near to them in the company. Then this was expanded because people saw they could use this to send packages to areas where fellow Globers lived. Just recently we had a big flood in a city in which we operate. Sadly fifty people died. The app allowed us to find Globers who were affected by the tragedy."

WHAT ABOUT YOU? WHO ARE YOU?

"I came from a family of entrepreneurs and the conversations around our home table were never about who I was going to work for, it was more of a case of what was I going to create. Supported by a loving family, there is no doubt this had an influence on my choices in life.

Many years ago I was involved in a serious car crash. According to the doctor, I had a 5 per cent chance of survival. It made me think a little deeper about why I'm here, the reason for it all. But I had no doubt I was here for a reason. I was saved for a reason. Now my major motivation is to leave a legacy. I am currently the Vice President of Endeavor Argentina, a global foundation that helps improve the entrepreneurial ecosystem in emerging markets by selecting, helping and promoting high-impact entrepreneurship."

GLOBANT TAKEAWAYS

- It is never a bad time to start a company. This company began in a crisis.
- The founding team had a mix of complementary skills.
- They had a dream with no business plan and limited working capital.
- Started by leveraging their friends.
- Values playing a major part in shaping the culture.
- A company is a social lab.
- Entrepreneurship requires hard work but not magic.
- Dream big and, after each achievement, dream bigger.
- Be extremely passionate, this is the journey of your life.

OUTFIT 7 – LIMASSOL, CYPRUS

My colleague Ksenja told me about Outfit 7 from Slovenia, creators of Talking Tom. Up until then I'd seen first-hand the joy and fun this interactive app had given our son Conor. Casual research revealed almost everyone I knew had the app and it didn't stop there.

Over one billion people from every demographic and niche market around the world have downloaded Outfit 7's apps. Talking Tom is one of the most popular apps on the planet. How did they do it?

Co-founders Iza and Samo share, "In the beginning there were eight founder members, seven males and one female. At the start they were all geeks but the characters have helped develop their personalities over time. We provided the finance and the other six founders left a search engine company to join us on the venture. We had no fear and believed we could succeed. The challenge was to find the route to success. Talking Tom was the answer.

While planning it, we started from the user point of view not from the business perspective. So we brainstormed on the product and when this part was finished, we started working on how to make money out of it. Talking Tom was indeed a classic example of xceptional execution of an ordinary idea. Fun was our x-factor, our xceptional ingredient. This is the direct result of the fun the developer had while working on the project. Indeed both of them are the same. You can't have one without the other. The original Talking Tom wasn't done in 3D so technology certainly wasn't the x-factor. Fun is one of our most important business values and you know this the minute you enter our company. How? It's easy. You hear our employees laughing.

The culture of the company is very much influenced by the characters. We try to have a family fun feel. If people aren't having fun it is impossible to infuse characters with it. We work very hard on this. Recruitment is critical in this context. Of course people come from different business cultures and we need to get them aligned to ours. We have a cultural advisor and an external psychologist who interview based on our values."

WHAT WAS LIFE LIKE BEFORE TALKING TOM?

"Before the idea was conceived, we researched the market a lot. Initially we wanted to bring out a 'useful' app, maybe a sport or an edutainment app that could help people – one that allowed parents to see where their children were at any time., but that market was saturated. More research highlighted that people don't necessary want the most useful apps, they want to be entertained. We chose this path, which allowed us to be creative, and an app was the medium as we felt games were also saturated. When Samo presented the Talking Tom concept to the team we were very skeptical about its possibilities but trusted and supported his vision. Our assessment was a little off the mark."

WHAT WERE THE SUCCESS FACTORS?

"When you develop an app and the company hasn't got strong brand awareness; you need to use a name that is instantly recognizable and easy to explain so you don't have to spend lots of money. Thus the app was called Talking Tom (Tom Cat).

Starting off is a major challenge when you are trying to promote and make it viral. You can focus on spending lots of money on banner adverts, which wasn't for us, or you can look at cross-promotion. The latter is where you use advertising on your own products to promote other apps. We worked hard to make sure it isn't seen as advertising. Moreover it is presented as useful content. If you flash adverts in front of users, it can be seen as too intrusive and turns customers off.

When we launched it in 2010 without advertising, it shot to the top of the app charts outside the US in a week. We then invested $6,000 in advertising pushing us to the top of the US equivalent. This type of success at that type of budget wouldn't be possible today. Today we have approximately 50 million downloads a month. The figure which got us to the top of the charts when it was launched, was much, much smaller. As you can imagine, as the use of smartphones has exploded, the market has too."

HOW MUCH DID IT COST TO DEVELOP?

"In terms of app development cost, it really depends on what way you look at it. If you look at it from the perspective of the amount of investment in the firm up to the launch, the figure was $200,000. If, on the other hand, reviewing just the time spent focusing on that exact project, probably of the order of $25,000."

WHAT WAS THE TARGET AUDIENCE?

"We have a wide spectrum of users for the app. The age profile goes from 9 months to 99 years. 3 to 35 years is the main demographic, split evenly between males and females. Children use the app as a nanny. Adults use it as a party trick. The elderly may use it for entertainment when they are on their own. But amazingly since launch we have received many emails from parents of autistic and Down Syndrome children and even people who are caring for people with Parkinson's disease. In the latter situation, by talking to the app, they can see that their voice is a little too low. So they then make a bigger effort when they are projecting. It is great that so many people have found purpose in the app. Of course if they don't, they will never return to it."

HOW DO YOU MONETIZE AN APP?

"The main route in the future is through licensing. This is why we have invested a lot of time and effort into character development. The most important thing is that the characters are likeable and loved by all ages from all parts of the globe. Our intention is to penetrate other media not just the mobile platform. When people like the brand they should be able to get it everywhere not just on your mobile. That is why we have developed a few videos with Disney. Apps can be copied, so the real challenge is to get into people's hearts with your characters. Yes for sure, Angry Birds has been an amazing success. One of the differences though is that we have concentrated a lot on our characters."

DO YOU TAKE TIME FOR TIMEOUT?

"We often go running in the morning and this is the time we get the best and the craziest ideas. Normally time is taken for a short meditation or preparation for that day on the top of the cliff above the sea. We really miss it if we're not in Cyprus. And there are many instant techniques you can use to boost yourself with the energy from the Universe."

NEW IDEAS IN THE PIPELINE?

"We have monthly meetings with time allotted for what we describe as pitching days or brainstorming etc. We encourage employees to share their ideas on a regular basis. We had to put some effort into explaining to them that there are millions of ideas every day for our products and only few of them make the cut. When they really understand that, contribution isn't a problem any more.

We are continually working on new ideas, some of which have huge potential for success. But you never know. Big news coming as we speak on Talking Tom. There is a TV series in the making for the Talking family. And finally a new app – an edutainment one for Ginger."

WHAT ABOUT PERSONAL DEVELOPMENT AND BUSINESS?

"There is no private and business life. It's only life. The knowledge can be equally used in private as well as in business life. The rules are exactly the same: if you can make the headache go away, you can make the app more successful. We are 22 years married. We got married early while studying and working on a project that helped preschoolers to read. We didn't work together for 15 years after that. When we did psychological testing we discovered we were opposites. It hasn't being a challenge working and living together. Because it is built on respect and a love of what we do and our extended family – Tom, Angela, Ben and Ginger. Of course in addition to the two people at the top believing in personal development and self-awareness, it must be the right vibe throughout the organization. We can highlight its importance, but it's up to people to choose to buy into it or not."

WHAT IS YOUR PERSPECTIVE ON MONEY?

"The thing in business is to understand and respect money. The money we get is only the energy we put into "it" in a different form. If we don't respect money, we don't respect our energy, we don't respect ourselves. Guilt about money comes from a time when people believed that only dedicated (holy) people had right to have more, to be happy etc. There is no need for this. Everybody has a right to be successful, to be happy, to be paid for the energy they put into the project. Money is not a dirty word or something we should be ashamed of."

VISION STATEMENT

"We are creating a better world in which the entertainment consumers of today rightly become the ultimate creators of tomorrow, empowered by our global cast of characters delighting people with joy, originality and unbound self-expression. We are surpassing all expectations and becoming the world's most creative, fun and successful entertainment outfit."

OUTFIT7 TAKEAWAYS

- Fun can be the x-factor.
- Look inside to find the sources of your fear.
- Sometime you can't see success in front of your eyes. You may be surprised by the impact your product or service will have.
- Make your app your customer's best friend.
- Invest in characters and bring them to life.
- Money, money – If you work hard, you deserve to be paid.
- There isn't a magic wand, but you must have the right people around you and aligned to your values.
- Listen and learn from criticism.
- Know thy customer.

UNISLIM – NEWRY, NORTHERN IRELAND

I was commissioned to do a keynote for Unislim Leaders by the existing CEO, Fiona Gratzner. At the event I was approached by the founder and Fiona's mother, Agnes McCourt, then a 72-year old fireball who was still running a class in Newry, County Down. She inspired me with her passion and genuine desire to see people improve their eating habits. This passion burns very brightly even after 40 years in the business. My mother attended these classes. When we spoke, Agnes shared the story of their very first class, one in which she admitted to having no clue whatsoever about the business. I was hooked.

Agnes McCourt recalls, "I was 42lbs overweight after the birth of my third child. I desperately wanted to shed the pounds and the only advice forthcoming from the doctor was to take slimming pills. After some deliberation and inspiration from my husband Brian, I decided to take action and invite friends and neighbors to my first Agnes McCourt Weight Reduction Class. The local priest gave us the hall and even got us our first three clients. These three plus six others turned up and so the journey began."

HOW PREPARED WERE YOU FOR YOUR FIRST CLASS?

"At the first class, I conceded to the audience that I hadn't much of a clue about weight loss. To start, I invited ladies to discuss their eating habits. They agreed on a confidentiality clause to ensure that what was said at the meeting stayed there. One lady put her hand up to inform all present that she ate a loaf of bread and pot of strawberry jam every day. Engaging my logical brain I suggested that the lady should try and cut that by half and see what happens. The following week the lady had lost two 2lbs. In the first week most of them lost weight. My advice was working. Three years later and three and a half stones lost in the process, the word started to hit the street that if you wanted to lose weight, I was the woman. 'She could talk the weight out of you'

On May 30, 1972, with the inspiration and direction of my husband, I started Unislim, a name that popped into my husband's mind one dark night in South Armagh. We were a superb team, I was very much the visionary and Brian was the person who took care of the details on the road to the goal. He was the research guru crafting speeches for the leaders on dietary and relevant topics and using his first class honors pedigree to conduct the most up-to-date and pertinent research. Bit by bit our cocktail of dieting advice, some exercise and community building initiative started to gain traction all around the country."

WHAT INFLUENCE DID YOUR UPBRINGING HAVE ON YOUR BUSINESS ACUMEN?

"I was the third of nine children and was brought up with a strong work ethic. From a very early age, I had to execute the various expected chores around a farm on a weekly basis – anything from milking the cow, delivering the lambs, cleaning the sheds, you name it, I did it. It taught me the importance of taking personal action, an understanding that gave me the courage and perseverance during the darker moments of life.

My father was a cattle dealer so wheeling and dealing was in the blood. My mother was very much the carer, always conscientious and reaching out, helping the less well off in the vicinity. Despite my entrepreneurial upbringing, I ended up in a permanent and pensionable teaching post, married to another teacher. Maybe those hours spent teaching the younger children in our house convinced me this was the career choice.

When we started Unislim Brian decided to give up his teaching job to focus 100 percent on what appeared to be a very big business opportunity. His decision wasn't welcomed by his mother, who wanted him to stay with his safe job. It took her a further 18 months before she could engage me in conversation again."

WHEN DID IT CLICK – THIS COULD BE BIG?

"At our first class in Warrenpoint under the Unislim brand we attracted 58 people. The attendance was overwhelming. That night I spoke to Brian's brother who posed an intriguing question – "What happens when everyone in Warrenpoint loses weight?' Not long after, that question prompted the following written response recorded on a piece of paper, "I am going to have a Unislim class in every town in Ireland.

This was my clear and compelling vision. I was convinced I could make it happen. Not everyone shared the same conviction. When I told Brian he thought I was crazy. At that time, apart from a possible visit to bingo in the week, the woman's place was firmly at home. There were no gyms or slimming classes so very few left their four walls to socialize. Unislim was to provide a new option. The early seventies in Northern Ireland offered another challenge, the Troubles, which were to have a profound effect on our life."

RECRUITMENT STRATEGY?

"In the context of recruiting new leaders, the decision is very much based on how I feel about the person. This is information I get from the gut. If it doesn't feel right, it isn't right. The Unislim company philosophy is something we take very seriously: To serve our members with enthusiasm and excellence, to provide the highest standard of service in our field and to improve the quality of life for all our members. If our leaders don't live and breathe this philosophy, I would have no hesitation in firing them on the spot. Remember for me not giving it all is like putting your hand in someone's pocket and taking their money."

HOW IMPORTANT ARE VALUES?

"Values are also a key driver in my life and decisions. My three main values are honesty, integrity and trust. Again in terms of employee selection and retention, if any of these three values are violated, the contract is immediately terminated. I never worked for money, I wanted to help people but I knew if I did a great job I would be well rewarded. Don't think there is a quick way to make lots of money. You have to have a passion, a love for what you do. I don't think it is sustainable otherwise. I still get upset when I see overweight people because they are not just ruining their own quality of life. It is likely they will pass this onto the generations that follow."

WHAT'S YOUR TAKE ON XCEPTIONAL EXECUTION?

"When you leave a class with a smile on your face, that's xceptional execution. A smile on your face means I have done a super job, I have given my all, done my best, that's xceptional execution. If your best isn't enough, look for a new business venture or job.

UNISLIM TAKEAWAYS

- Retirement is not an option.
- Is work ethic in your genes?
- If you can find a solution to a problem, go for it.

- No knowledge required.
- Persevere – don't mind if you get the odd door slammed in your face.
- You won't please all the people all of the time.
- Be fearless in the face of injustice.
- Money follows a job well done.
- No 'buts' when you are recruiting.
- If your best isn't enough, look for a new business venture or job.

WEDEMAND (QUEREMOS) – RIO DE JANEIRO, BRAZIL

My colleague in Brazil, Fabiano, introduced me to a funding agency that considered WeDemand.com as one of the jewels in their portfolio. I love the concept and the story behind it. Five music-loving boys from Brazil wanted to see their favorite bands in their home city. They built an innovative business around the solution they found. There's a rawness about their story and Bruno's passion and excitement for this venture is refreshing and infectious. Their story shows the magic, adventure and huge learning curve of an early stage start-up.

WHAT IS XCEPTIONAL EXECUTION?

Bruno Natal explains, "xceptional execution is something that is good for everyone. It balances all the parts of the process. The customers are happy because they get at worst a discounted ticket but potentially a free one to their chosen concert. The band is happy because the platform allows them to see and satisfy demand in cities they may never have thought about visiting. The promoter is happy because the crowdsourcing aspect takes the risk out of bringing the band to the venue."

HOW DID IT ALL BEGIN?

"The company and the crowdsourcing idea came out of the necessity of solving a group of true music fans' problem. The genesis of this idea was that a promoter had the possibility of bringing an act to Rio de Janeiro but was worried about the risks involved. It was one of the co-founder's favorite bands and they pondered how they could make it happen.

The deposit involved was $10,000 and one of the guys believed it was possible to email 120 of their friends and get 100 of them to make an investment of $100 each, hence securing the $10,000 deposit. The investors knew if the concert was advertised in the open market and it sold well, then they would make their money back and of course enjoy the concert and their part therein for free. In a stadium that held 2,000 people, 1,000 people turned up. The fans got their money back and we made a little profit.

We knew that promoters were always concerned about booking bands for Rio. The natives never decide to book for a concert until the day of the gig. If it has been hot all day, they may decide to stay at home. If it was raining, this would also result in a no show. Add in a lack of buzz around town about an event, then as a promoter you were really worried about the outcome. That is why so many music lovers had to travel to Sao Paulo to see their favorite bands at a huge cost. Plane ticket, accommodation and concert ticket cost could run into a few hundred dollars. The alternative we wanted to create was paying $100 – expensive, yet cheaper than the current option."

WHAT WERE CUSTOMERS DEMANDING?

"After a while the model changed. Early investors were allowed tickets at a discounted rate and if the venue sold out they would enjoy the experience for free. What's more the take up was significant for another reason – people were thrilled to be part of something xceptional, to be the reason this event happened. This, plus the obvious benefits of enjoying their favorite band at a discount price, made the investment an unmissable opportunity.

The cost in some way became secondary to this far-reaching buying experience. After conducting two further pieces of research – one answered by more than 6k users and a focus group – we confirmed that the refund is not what motivates people. Making a concert happen does. So now we are going to reward the most frequent users with free tickets within a loyalty program."

WERE PEOPLE CONCERNED ABOUT THEIR MONEY?

Trust was an important factor in building the business. People needed to be confident in us to part with their money. My own profile generated from my column in the second biggest paper in Brazil, O Globo, and blog helped in this respect. The internet in a way has been the catalyst for increased transparency in business and that is good."

DID YOU HAVE A CLEAR VIEW OF WHERE YOU WERE GOING FROM DAY 1?

"At the outset there was no vision or business plan. Things evolved in line with the demands placed on us by others. For example, the business plan was done when we were seeking investment. The company was self-funded to start with, living off some of the profits of the organized events. The majority of the profits was continually reinvested. Then in December we joined 20121.com and raised $900,000. All the other four co-founders are full time – I am the only one who has still got other small interests – my blog and column."

DISRUPTIVE OR COLLABORATIVE?

"Today we aren't trying to be disruptive. Indeed the idea is to be more of a collaborative platform. We see it evolving more into a platform for the interested parties, more so than us organizing events on our own. It will be a platform where a promoter can assess the potential demand in an area and know from the information that they should be going for a 2,000 seat capacity rather than the intended 1,000 and so on. The artists will benefit from increased dates, but even more importantly a better quality of contact with their fans."

HOW IMPORTANT WERE YOUR FRIENDSHIPS IN BUILDING THE BUSINESS?

"Four of the five co-founders know each other from their

college days when we either locked horns on the football pitch or collaborated on a literature fanzine. The final director, Pedro, became friendly with me when I was completing my Masters in Documentary Film Making in London in 2007. I invited him on board. Each of us has a unique and relevant experience. Tiago Lins, an economist who used to have an Indie band some years back, is now the Chief Financial Officer. Felipe Continentino was in advertising and is now our COO. I was a journalist and am now the communications guy. Pedro Seiler is the A and R Music Researcher and Pedro Garcia is Chief of Products."

HOW DID YOU INVEST YOUR RESOURCES?

"After receiving the funding we were in a position to employ three programmers, a social media manager, and for the first time in two and a half years, pay ourselves a wage. In addition, lots of work was carried out on the site. The US market was also targeted. Much bigger and well established, it has many players and all with their places in the chain secure. We are trying to add something that would benefit everyone, so the main job right now is to accommodate opinions and requests without losing sight of who we are and what we do. One of the co-founders has moved to New York to build the business there. This takes time as you try to build relationships with promoters and build buzz around the brand. We were fortunate in Brazil as we had much more recognition at the beginning because of our work and presence here. In the USA we were starting from scratch."

HOW DO YOU GAIN TRACTION?

"The good thing is that people have been very receptive to the idea and that is encouraging. We are getting good press and some of the artists are talking about it in their social media circles – Snoop Dog [Lion] and T Mills. There have been copycats, particularly on home turf, but I believe they underestimated the importance of relationships and time. It is a bit more complicated than just what they see on the site. "

DO YOU SWITCH OFF?

"No, even less now, because it is a very sensitive time. Music is our love. We are all music fans so for me definitely, I would do it for nothing just to be involved. We are still super excited. But we haven't got any time to be dreaming as most of us are consumed with the demands of each day."

WHAT IS YOUR SELLING STRATEGY?

"Every time we have a campaign people engage and the word spreads. We have concerts and more people learn about WeDemand.com, and it keeps on going like that. We are very driven to do what we are setting out to do in a clear and honest way. Every single day, the main focus of the whole operation is on how to keep putting the customers first."

WEDEMAND TAKEAWAYS

- Don't make finding a solution a goal. Find a problem first, especially one that you experience yourself.
- Satisfying a customer's need for significance could be your unique selling point.
- Execution dampens fears.
- The power of friendships to build a business.
- No need for a plan, vision or values – just DO!
- Word of mouth both online and off is a powerful tool.
- Time for timeout in early start-up days can be a challenge, but passion can see you through.
- Never stop focusing on developing a rich customer experience.

ABOUT THE AUTHOR

Kevin is a leading authority on the success principles of entrepreneurship, leadership, sales and motivation. Raised among a small entrepreneurial family retail business, he has been selling and negotiating, listening to and serving customers from a very young age. After graduating from University College Galway with a Bachelor of Commerce degree in 1987, he proceeded to break sales records in each of the companies he worked for in the construction and manufacturing industries. In 1990 he started his company, Advanced Marketing Ltd.

Kevin coined the phrase 'xceptionalize' which challenges organizations and individuals to focus upon the xceptional execution of those activities that really contribute most to success.

His previous publications include the best-selling titles *Basics before Buzz, How? When you don't know how, Life – a Trip Towards Trust* and *Xceptionalize – Success Secrets for Students.* He has also produced three audio books *Compelling Communication Strategies, Setting, getting and forgetting goals* and *Good enough – now go get it.* Kevin demonstrates the power of cultivating an ROI – return on intuition.

Kevin actively keynotes at corporate meetings and conferences throughout Europe, the Middle East, Asia and the Americas, from Tehran to Monaco, Hong Kong to Bogota, Seoul to Colorado, addressing Fortune 500 companies, The Million Dollar Round Table, Chambers of Commerce and investment funds amongst many other groups in IT, Pharmaceuticals, Healthcare, Financial Services and Retail. In the prevailing attention deficit society high levels of engagement are achieved through a unique interactive cocktail of exercises, stories, the most up to date research and original content. Your team will be challenged, informed, and inspired.

KEYNOTES

Kevin's dynamic keynotes are a catalyst for organizational optimization and xceptional execution. He delivers an interactive experience that inspires, challenges and informs audiences, drawing on his diverse entrepreneurial, corporate and life experiences, including hard won insights into human behavior. Implementing the best practices of the world's xceptionalists will enhance your employee and customer engagement and propel profits.

Start-ups: Developing the Xceptionalist mindset

Aspiring entrepreneurs face many challenges before taking that vital first step, not least the intimidating myths that they must be a stand-out visionary, have a breakthrough unique idea and work to a detailed, all-worked-out-in-advance business plan.

Furthermore, according to the Global Entrepreneurial Monitor, deep inside themselves is a fear of failure, cited as the number one reason why people fail to act upon their entrepreneurial dreams and ideas. This energy packed, mind-recharging keynote will unlock the fear factor and dispel the myths holding people back.

- No need to wait for an 'aha' moment before starting.
- Solving a personal problem may be your next blockbuster business idea.
- Failing to plan is planning to succeed.
- Seeing, not solving the problem is your greatest challenge.
- Fear as a positive influence.
- Building friendships is the route to a sustainable business.
- Past strategies inform the future.

SMEs and Solopreneurs – Business growth through xceptional execution

In 2000 leading research by Professor Amar Bhide from Colombia University in his book The age and evolution of business identified that 88% of the breakthrough USA companies over the previous decade were the result of 'xceptional execution of an ordinary idea'. Kevin unpacks the thinking behind those who live and breathe the xceptional execution mindset and approach to business and life, revealing the key elements required to create a culture of xceptional execution.

- Culture begins and ends with leadership.
- Strategy acknowledges an attention deficit market.
- Selling back the customers product.
- Make active listening your unique selling point.
- Move away from building traditional relationships.
- Sales team evolves in composition and competency.
- Manage those moments.

Leaders and intrapreneurs – Lead like an xceptionalist

In 2007 Stanford Business Advisory Council highlighted self-awareness as the most important attribute a leader should develop. In 2011 an IBM study cited staying close to the customer as the most important strategy for business leaders. In this keynote, Kevin expands upon these insights by highlighting how to mirror the mindset, attitudes and success strategies of the outstanding xceptionalists he interviewed for his book *DO! the pursuit of xceptional execution*.

- Developing an authentic presence and empowering culture.
- Complicated people are incredibly predictable.
- Communicating in clutter.
- The power of friendships.
- ROI – return on intuition.
- See value in values and show patience in vision.
- A culture of paranoia.